Jung, Buddhism,
and the
Incarnation of Sophia

"That Henry Corbin was one of the great religious thinkers of the 20th century will be apparent to all who delve into this brilliant collection of his previously unpublished writings on Carl Jung and Buddhism, the gnostic Sophia, and Sufism. Corbin's insights into the profound roots of Jung's teachings make this essential reading for those who ponder the ties that bind psychology and spirituality and all the great religious traditions to one another."

JEFF ZALESKI, EDITOR AND PUBLISHER
OF *PARABOLA* MAGAZINE

"Jung, Buddhism, and the Incarnation of Sophia is where two astounding explorers of the inner cosmos, Henri Corbin and Carl Jung, meet in their insights—an intriguing octagon of mirrors surrounding the illuminated soul."

CHRIS H. HARDY, PH.D., AUTHOR OF
THE SACRED NETWORK, DNA OF THE GODS,
AND *WARS OF THE ANUNNAKI*

Jung, Buddhism,

and the

Incarnation

of Sophia

Unpublished Writings from the Philosopher of the Soul

Henry Corbin

Edited by Michel Cazenave

with the assistance of Daniel Proulx

Translated by Jack Cain

Inner Traditions

Rochester, Vermont

Inner Traditions
One Park Street
Rochester, Vermont 05767
www.InnerTraditions.com

Copyright © 2014 by Éditions Entrelacs
English translation copyright © 2019 by Inner Traditions International

Originally published in French under the title *Autour de Jung: Le bouddhisme et la Sophia* by Éditions Entrelacs, 19, rue Saint-Séverin 75005 Paris
First U.S. edition published in 2019 by Inner Traditions

Cataloging-in-Publication Data for this title is available from the Library of Congress

ISBN 978-1-62055-739-6 (print)
ISBN 978-1-62055-740-2 (ebook)

Printed and bound in the United States by Versa Press, Inc.

10 9 8 7 6 5 4 3 2

Text design and layout by Priscilla Baker
This book was typeset in Garamond Premier Pro with Avenir, Legacy Sans, and Minion used as display typefaces

Nous tenons à exprimer nos plus vifs remerciements au gouvernement de la France et au ministère de la Culture, Centre National du Livre, pour leur concours dans la préparation de la traduction de cet ouvrage.

Contents

PART I

Carl Gustav Jung and Buddhism

PART II
ANSWER TO JOB

APPENDICES

PREFACE
FROM THE EDITOR

I am publishing these documents just as Stella Corbin kindly entrusted them to me. And specifically in the form in which she suggested they be presented.

Readers will not then be surprised to find two pieces by me that open and close this volume—something that I would never have undertaken on my own—but, once again, the publication entrusted to me has required me to do so!

In the same way, I know quite well—and Daniel Proulx (a religious and philosophical scholar specializing in Henry Corbin's thinking) pointed it out to me at length—that Corbin's study of the connections between Jung and Buddhism (Buddhism as it was presented by D. T. Suzuki) has been organized in various ways. I decided on this point to conform strictly to the manuscript that was typed by his own hands and provided to me by Mrs. Corbin, so that I would be respecting her wish to publish this research together with Corbin's various texts on the aspects of Sophia that are found in Jung's work.

Regarding also the documents appearing in the appendices, which she gave me with specific instructions as to their placement: I know very well that the sequencing of this collection could be contested, but I would like it to be understood that, if I bring to light and put forward these facts, it is certainly not in a spirit of trying to place elsewhere the responsibility for any part of it but simply to delineate a faithful adherence imposed by the passing of the person whom we are dealing with here.

Finally, I cannot end without recognizing once again the invaluable collaboration of Daniel Proulx who not only gave me the necessary encouragement, but above all supported the proper publication of these texts through his painstaking research in storage boxes of Corbin archives at the École pratique des hautes études.*

MICHAEL CAZENAVE

MICHEL CAZENAVE (June 9, 1942–August 20, 2018) was a French philosopher and an expert on the work of Carl Jung. He was a prolific writer with more than fifty books to his credit and was longtime advisor to the head of programming for the prestigious France Culture, a French public radio channel featuring historical, philosophical, sociopolitical, and scientific content.

---

*The École pratique des hautes études was established in the Sorbonne in 1868. It provides lectures and undertakes research in life and earth sciences, historical and philological sciences, and religious sciences. —*Trans.*

Henry Corbin, Philosopher of the Soul

Michel Cazenave

It will soon be three years since Henry Corbin departed this life.* His excessive modesty as a researcher and thinker perhaps prevented him during his lifetime from occupying his legitimate position at the horizon of French thought—and doubtless beyond: European thought and Western thought as well. An enormous misunderstanding developed around him: as an orientalist for the philosophers and a philosopher for the orientalists, no one quite knew where to place him, nor was it understood that it was moreover this very indefinable character that doubtlessly legitimized the unfolding of his work. And his work was specifically elsewhere than at the philosophical dead end in which we have been imprisoned now for nearly fifty years.

Philosopher in actual fact, Henry Corbin was indeed that to the very depths of his soul—and I use the word *soul* deliberately, because Corbin had quite rightly understood, and was among the first to understand, that a philosophy of being was also, and necessarily so,

*This preface was written in 1981. Henry Corbin died in 1978. —*Trans.*

1

a philosophy that posited the rigorous reality of the soul. Several of Corbin's books have recently appeared one after the other: *Temple et contemplation (Temple & Contemplation;* Flammarion, 1980), *Le Paradoxe du monothéisme* (The paradox of monotheism; L'Herne, 2003), *La Philosophie iranienne islamique aux xviie et xviiie siècles* (Islamic Iranian philosophy of the seventeenth and eighteenth centuries; Buchet-Castel, 1994), as well as the monumental and, for the foreseeable future, indispensable *Cahier de l'Herne: Henry Corbin* (Herne notebooks: Henry Corbin; L'Herne, 1981) edited by Christian Jambet.

This outpouring of published works is meaningful in itself. If Corbin's thought has really not yet reached a wide audience, I have often been led to realize how it has been influencing more and more, and more and more deeply, new generations of young philosophers— or researchers—those seeking knowledge in the neighboring domains of psychology and anthropology; for example, where Corbin provides them with operative conceptual tools. The time has come today for such a magnetic pole to break the wall of silence so the fruits of an entire life devoted to the search for Knowledge might flood restless souls with Light.

It has been a long time—a very long time now—that Western philosophy has split at its very core and given rise to two antithetical pairs that are connected by their respective terms: intellectualism and empiricism, idealism and materialism. The result we can see then is the wall that present-day philosophy is up against, the dead end it has come to, and its dramatic inability to bridge the divisions that it has itself created. This philosophy has come to a place where the reality of the soul, in its turn, has sunk; it has been emptied of any possibility of existing within the pitiless struggle between the world's opacity and endless concepts.

It is specifically this fratricidal struggle that Henry Corbin wants to go beyond, and he does so by rising above it in such a way that dogmatisms shatter and ideologies fall from the false thrones they have accorded themselves. Within the kingdom of the soul thus reconquered, as an intermediate world between our perceivable universe and the divine unintelligible, there can finally develop—or be redeveloped—a philosophy of the Active Imagination, which has been in all ages that of true mystics, poets with hearts aflame, lovers, and those crazed with God.

It is in fact patently clear that official Western philosophy has failed in its mission, which was to think Being. Because, if Being "is," it is clearly of absolute transcendence—and to skirt this obstacle, metaphysics has all too often positioned, at the core of its thinking, a supreme Be-er, an extreme Exister if you like, which when all is said and done is an *idol,* instead of this absolute God the source of which all thirsty souls are searching for. "On my bed, at nighttime, I sought him whom my heart loves"*—to which respond the words of Teresa of Ávila in her poem "Aspirations toward Eternal Life": "I live without living within myself, / and in such a way I hope, / I die because I do not die."

Because the essential problem is right there for any real contemplative who tries to think about the relationship of man to being: How does one maintain transcendence in its proper aspect while at the same time allowing the soul to enjoy what that transcendence produces?

The Soul and Imagination

To respond to this project—and respond in a strictly philosophical way that is thoughtful and critical at the same time—there are, Corbin tells us, two essential conditions and a required method.

---

*Song of Songs 3:1. (Scripture is directly translated from the French; it is unknown which edition of the Bible Corbin used for his quotations. —*Trans.*)

The conditions are simple: We must restore to the soul its complete integrity, which is to say that we must definitively allow once again its intrinsic and undeniable reality, and that must be the place where the divine appears. From this, the second condition follows logically, which is to restore to *imagination* its status, which is to be a mediator between the world and God, between creation and the Creator. (But take care! It's not just any imagination and certainly not the *imaginary* that we usually designate by this term.)

This means moreover that the creature—that is, man in this case—avails himself of an Active Imagination, an imagination as agent that fills the space of the soul. By engendering its own world of visions and illumination, the soul rediscovers the too often forgotten angel as divine manifestation. The "interworld" created in this way was sought above all by Henry Corbin—this imaginal world, whose name he adopted from high medieval philosophy. It is a world where spirit is incarnated and the body is spiritualized, an interworld that we can also call, according to tradition, the world of subtle bodies or the world of bodies of glory. As for Henry Corbin, he sought this world in Iranian Islam and in Sufi and Shi'ite mysticism from Ibn 'Arabi in Andalusia to Suhrawardi in Persia.

However, it is important not to think that he was intent on leaving the West behind. In fact, quite the contrary I am sure. It is simply the case that in the history of philosophy it is the Iranian mystics and thinkers who ventured along this path and therefore mapped or "delimited" the land as was done by the explorers of unknown continents in the past two or three centuries.

A Real Ecumenism

Now Corbin's concern has always been that of a real ecumenism that builds bridges between the spiritual flowerings of different traditions from the moment that they did not devour the Divine in History. Thus, respecting a plurality of meanings, they kept the soul in its domain, which ought to be that of making a connection between secular history and the Being in Being itself. "Philosophy," said Jambet, in speaking of this enormous task, "is a logic of being which becomes transformed into a burning in the soul, within the luminous love of the angel."

In this research program experienced as a mixture of erudition and contemplation, there is thus a new career opening in Western thought, which is revivifying it both from the inside and from the outside. (Let us not forget Denys, Scotus Erigena, and certain flashes of insight in Leibniz.) It is in this way that a new philosophy is being built that is no longer in contradiction with or foreign to spirituality, but which rather is essential to it and which, while proclaiming its autonomy, helps spirituality not to fall into already set traps of facile sentimentality or of being reduced to History, which ends up emptying religious reality of all its meaning.

La Croix, France,
May 1981

PART I

CARL GUSTAV JUNG AND BUDDHISM

Publisher's Note on Sources and Corbin's Commentary

As noted in the preface by Michel Cazenave, these pages are presented as they were passed on to him by Henry Corbin's wife, Stella—including the order of the material as well as unfinished asides and musings from the author. As part 1 of this book was never published prior to Corbin's death, there are a number of unpolished or unifinished reflections, becoming more and more frequent throughout part 1. These are indicated in parenthesis in *the italic font shown here.*

Most of Corbin's original sources were in German, as Jung's work had not been translated at the time Corbin was writing. The French edition of his work updated citations to French editions of the German texts where possible. For our readership we have further updated citations to English editions where possible, or else returned the citation to the author's original German source.

Notes from Michel Cazenave, the editor of the French edition, have been clearly indicated as such, as have notes from the English translator to distinguish from Corbin's own notes.

All of this was done in an effort to preserve insights into the author's private musings as well as to ensure a clear and smooth reading experience.

INTRODUCTION TO PART I

The sequence of the four studies is a meditative order—simply one possible choice. They could have been presented in another order. It is not in any way a rational systematization. The invisible connecting thread guiding us here was the condition of Awakening as found in the Buddhism of the Great Vehicle (Mahāyāna Buddhism).* We found this condition presented in the most striking way—even a most (literally) brutal way. The connecting thread had us study as well the training that must prepare for that Awakening and the exercises that must extend the results of it to every perspective of life and to the things of life. Every sphere of consciousness must be penetrated, ceaselessly reactivating the Awakening, while at the same time keeping in the awareness, from the sphere of transcendence, the energy which in the first place abruptly transformed the student's mode of being and of seeing.

A few years ago in a country that is for the most part an Islamic land, I had the occasion to give a talk on one of the great spiritual figures of Sufism. Perhaps it was that a scholarly man, for whom learning would be in vain without the experience of the heart, had heard about the talk on this occasion. What followed a few days later was that I was

---

*To properly understand what is at stake, we must recall that Corbin is speaking of Buddhism as it was often presented in the Ascona meetings in the Italian-speaking region of Switzerland by D. T. Suzuki. —*Ed.*

visited by two young men who came to "interview" me on behalf of their master who was a great enemy of Sufism—one of these strange personages about whom one cannot be sure whether they are fanatically modern or whether their "modernism" isn't an especially "modern" fanaticism. They were alarmed enough to probe the aim that I was pursuing. Was I something of a historian, or was I a kind of religious agitator or reformer? A concern for truth required me to explain that history as such did not interest me. Delineating what a spiritual greatness manifested in the past means for us "in the present" is doing something other than history. And at the same time, the feeling of my own strengths required me to confess that I had no aptitude for the role of reformer. I tried to explain that I was doing "phenomenology." But it was radically impossible to translate the word and the concept directly into my visitors' language, let alone evoke in a few sentences what such a word can mean for us, what transformation it induces in the state of our problems, and what perspectives it overturns in our consciousness. I watched a kind of mounting stupor in the two young men, as if, faced by these incomprehensible words, they were realizing that the situation was even worse than they could have ever imagined. I do not know if afterward their master's worries continued—as it happened, the poor man was assassinated a few months later.

This experience allowed me to measure to what extent, in such a milieu of a given spiritual culture, it is difficult to propose to an audience or to an individual an exchange on a spiritual subject without speaking either in a historical mode or in a dogmatic mode. The first offers you comfortable excuses—you are interesting and curious but in the past and therefore inoffensive. The second puts you immediately into harmony with the collective norms of the audience chosen beforehand, and your situation is similarly inoffensive. When you try to reach the individual soul, to provoke in him the shock that may awaken him to himself, to the truth of his own being that is his alone to assume in this world, without any consideration of other interests than his personal destiny, which he must take on by himself, then in such a case your endeavor will turn out to be threatening for a whole heap of reasons, of which in your simplicity you did not suspect either the existence or the danger. Conversely, the call addressed to the individual with a view to an experience that must transform his whole mode of being and understanding, without targeting a profession of faith or a triumph of propaganda—such a call is one of the most striking traits in the teaching of Buddhism such as it is dispensed by a Suzuki. *(However, it is what is the most striking in the spiritual teaching of Buddhism. For Suzuki, sects. Then the passage by Jung, 32.)* The Buddhist sects coexist perfectly well without any of the denominational rivalries that weigh down our past. Would it then be the state of our spiritual culture that has not prepared, or foreseen or admitted, the call to "become oneself"? It would be a paradox to sustain this call. But it would not be a paradox to realize that anyone professing that such a call is the supreme "religious" goal for a human being will find himself at best not being understood and at worst denounced by the existing "religions"—especially those religions that have been "laicized," the result of pseudo-transformations that extend the misunderstanding, sometimes in political attire, sometimes under a so-called esotericism that is even more intransigent and dogmatic than the dogmas it claims to rise above.

Now, it is such a call and such a faith that we recognize in the teaching and practice of Carl Gustav Jung—the process of individuation. A passage such as the following formulates the reason and the consequences of his encounter with Buddhism: "I have no doubt the *satori experience* does occur also in the West, for we too have men who scent ultimate ends and will spare themselves no pains to draw near to them. But they will keep silence, not only out of shyness but because they know that any attempt to convey their experiences to others would be hopeless. For there is nothing in our culture approaching these aspirations, not even the Church, the custodian of religious goods. It is in fact her function to oppose all such extreme experiences, for these can only be heterodox. The only movement within our culture that partly has—and partly should have—some understanding of these aspirations is psychotherapy. It is therefore not a matter of chance that this foreword is written by a psychotherapist."* What motivates this passage of text is specifically the desire to illustrate this encounter with Buddhism.

---

*C. G. Jung's foreword to D. T. Suzuki, *An Introduction to Zen Buddhism,* New York, Grove Press, 1964, xxv; *Gesammelte Werke,* vol. 11, § 903.

1

ZEN

On *The Book of Great Deliverance*

An acquaintance with Zen Buddhism is accessible to Western readers in part thanks to the translations and admirable studies by Suzuki. We have all seen clearly that Zen is neither a psychology nor a philosophy in the senses that we usually give those words. The shock that Zen intends, operating within a soul—which then is transformed—comes to fruition in a totally irrational process, unconnected to the data and provisions of logic and dialectic. *(Perhaps a general overview on the use of the word* soul *here. Buddhist meaning. Jung's meaning. Synthesis between negation and negation of negation.)* The implications of this process, and the discovery that on completion creates the initial reality of a new mode of being and perception, are specifically what bring the Zen school of Buddhism and Jung's psychotherapy into harmonious relationship. We would like to take up this harmony here as the initial theme of our "paraphrase."

From the outset, we might wonder if such a theme doesn't tend toward a contradictory initiative. What forms the essence and raison d'être of Zen is the central intuition that is designated by the Japanese term *satori,* which we can attempt to translate by "enlightenment." Here we have a *mysterium ineffabile.* Between the famous and very strange anecdotes with their often absurd wording that Zen offers for contemplation by its adepts, and the enlightenment that blossoms abruptly and brutally, there yawns an abyss that cannot be bridged with rational contemplation or explanation. As Jung says,* all you can do is to maneuver through the neighboring proximity, and the maneuvering is all the more difficult because you are then going counter to the spirit of Zen. The impression that seems to emerge is one of an experience *a nihilo,* which corresponds to an inner movement of what in astrology or cosmology is called *creatio ex nihilo.* What rejects this, setting itself in opposition to emanationism, is specifically the train of thought that begins by positing something based on which there would be derived or emanated—necessarily—all the superabundance of being. This being said, we do not mean to imply that the creationist doctrines were aware of this—far from it. But instead: the legendary brutality with which certain famous Zen masters replied to their students' questions, by hitting them with their stick or their fist, responds to the necessity to create pure, naked fact, before and beyond all affirmation and all negation, before and beyond all preexisting material support on which it might repose. The explosion of an encounter, the injunction "Show me—or discover, or study—your face as it was before you were born, before the creation of the world." Absolute *initium. Urerfahrung.* Experience that is *ab initio* and *ab imo,* initial and of the void. That which supports the intuitive understanding of what the void (*śūnya*) is—this concept about which so many misunderstandings have arisen and which has led so superficially to talk of Buddhist "nihilism." It is a question of expunging from conscious-

---

*C. G. Jung's foreword to D. T. Suzuki, *An Introduction to Zen Buddhism* (New York: Grove Press, 1964); *Gesammelte Werke,* vol. 11, § 881, no. 8.

ness all representations of objects, the assemblage or configuration of which are imposed on consciousness as data that it sustains, as well as expunging along with those representations all the laws of physics and history. One must put oneself back to the origin, pierce through to the mind whose own law alone assembled these objects and their representations. And then, finding this original void, which is absolute power, the principle of contradiction will also have been surmounted, since things and beings once again will be there but in a transformed sense.

This is the sense of the very striking Image used by one of the masters whom Suzuki quotes: "Before a man studies Zen, mountains are mountains to him and waters are waters. But when he obtains a glimpse into the truth of Zen through the instruction of a good master, mountains are no longer mountains, nor waters waters; later, however, when he has really reached the place of Rest (that is, has attained satori), mountains are again mountains, and waters waters."*

The man who confronted the world of objects and the reality of objects was a man who was full of *himself*. What was this *himself* of which he was full and how, specifically, by giving way to illusion, does he "egoify" this "I"? How does he make it into ego by succumbing to the illusion of objects? An "I" that clearly has not been and could not have been set aside by a rational negation (that is, a negative, logical operation).

"If I came to see you with nothing, what would you say?"

"Drop it!"

"But I just told you I have nothing! How can I drop it?"

"So, pick it up!"

This nothing about which he has been thinking is still something

---

*Quoted in Jung's foreword to *Introduction to Zen Buddhism*, xiiin; *Gesammelte Werke*, vol. 11, § 884, no. 11.

affected by a negative sign, a nothing that is still rational, decreed by logic. It is not the void that is referred to by the teaching of the Great Vehicle, which is attained, "realized," through a shattering of the "I" that clamps on to rational consciousness—the consciousness that is like a blinding and a limitation of consciousness itself. The experience of satori is the emancipation from that, and, by discovering your face before the initial instant of the creation of things (where all things are created in front of you and through you—the pure Thus), it gives you access to the Pure Land of transcendent consciousness. There we have a totality of the consciousness of life. "The world of the mind encloses the whole universe in its light . . . it is a cosmic life and cosmic spirit, and at the same time an individual life and an individual spirit."*

This emancipation of consciousness, which frees itself from its servitude and its misfortune by recognizing the nonconscious immensity limiting it and oppressing it, is specifically the emancipation that all of Jung's psychotherapy specifically targets. Consciousness is limited and oppressed only as long as it refuses to recognize that immensity. The refusal of this recognition postulates the common confusion of the "I" with the "Self." Furthermore, no matter what definition we propose, the Self is other than the "I," and to the extent even where a higher or deeper penetration of the "I" takes one to the Self, it is that the latter is something more vast; its extent includes the experience of "I," and consequently goes beyond it. "In the same way as the *ego* is a certain knowledge of my *self,* so is the self a knowledge of my ego, which, however, is no longer experienced in the form of a broader or higher ego, but in the form of a non-ego (*Nicht-Ich*)."†

---

*Kaiten Nukariya, *The Religion of the Samurai: A Study of Zen Philosophy and Discipline in China and Japan* (London: Luzac, 1913), 132; quoted in Jung's foreword to *Introduction to Zen Buddhism,* xiii; *Gesammelte Werke,* vol. 11, § 884, no. 12.
†Jung's foreword to *Introduction to Zen Buddhism,* xiii; *Gesammelte Werke,* vol. 11, § 885.

The fourth text of Jung, which we are going to analyze later on, will show us more exactly, on the occasion of Jung's encounter with Buddhist meditation, the form assumed by the Self in his psychology. Without any doubt, one of the most attractive aspects of his immense body of work is how Jung outlines connections established among the data of experience. The constraints of our purely historical classifications and disciplines do not even allow us to approach this aspect. But, specifically, if these encounters are possible, if these "harmonizations" can be awakened, it follows that, from the outset, the question is posed because it has been made possible and is required by the premises! Is there among us in the West something that corresponds—closely or distantly—to the experience of satori? A question of such far-reaching resonance is something for which the conclusion of the Geleitwort can only suggest the outlines. In any case, to the extent that the event of satori is interpreted as the piercing of a consciousness formerly limited to its "egoified" "I" form (Ichform) and interpreted as opening access to the "non-egoified" "I" form of the Self (nicht-ichnaften Selbst), it is of prime importance to take note of its being identical to the teaching of Meister Eckhart—and specifically the extraordinary sermon of the master on the first beatitude: *Beati pauperes spiritu*—a long text in which Jung brings together images that are specifically identical to those familiar to Zen.* We must quote here in its entirety this long and admirable text.

> When I came out from God, all things said, "There is a God!" But that cannot make me blissful, for with it I conceive myself to be a creature. But in the break-through [. . .] I am neither God nor creature: *I am what I am, and what I will remain,* now and forever!

---

*Jung's foreword to *Introduction to Zen Buddhism,* xiv; *Gesammelte Werke,* vol. 11, § 887.

[. . .] I perceive what God and I are in common. [. . .] Here God no longer abides in man, for man through his poverty has won back what he has always been and will always be.*

And perhaps then we must say that if the Buddhist concept of the void seems to us at first so strange and leads to so many misunderstandings, the closest we can come in speaking of this concept in Western languages is that of this poverty found in Eckhart and in the Gospels. One way or another, the experience described is that of a satori, as a "stand-in" of the "I" by the Self. It is to the Self that there belongs the *buddhatā* (Japanese: *busshō*), the "Buddha nature."

Now, we would say that no doubt a little of this Eckhartian poverty will be needed to accept and draw profit from the way Jung intends to treat the issues here—that is, as psychological issues. We will even see in the end a retort to the trivial "It's only psychology"— and perhaps what is only destitution and poverty in the eyes of the philosopher and theologian will appear to us like the core of a richness that escapes them. In summary, it is a question of understanding how these apparently absurd dialogues preserved in Zen books have been able to lead to such complete changes in consciousness. Let us not stop at the pitiful excuse that is content to claim that it is a self-created suggestion. Because, here too, is not an "imaginary" pain often more painful, more intolerable, than a "real" pain? Does it not have its own reality whose sole criterion is specifically the person undergoing it? Right from the start, we are confronted by the demand that reappears throughout the whole body of this work of Jung—the psychologist who dared to speak of soul—the demand of psychic reality and psychic

*Quoted in Jung's foreword to *Introduction to Zen Buddhism*, xiv; *Gesammelte Werke*, vol. 11, § 887.

events.* This is why we say "spirit of poverty": because this reality of the soul is so tenuous, so fragile for modern man! Now here we affirm the primacy of that reality, allowing us to give up on the positive materiality of external, physical facts—such materiality cannot in any case furnish any criteria in determining whether an Enlightenment was real or imagined. After all, what kind of reality can it be if it were not "imagined" in the soul? Here we have a turning around of things such that, if this reality is implicated in satori, we would need to agree that, unless we take the path of our mystics, it will be difficult for us in the West to find any experience that corresponds to it.

A characterization of this turned-around view that is still partial could present it by substituting for the consciousness of the existence of an object, a consciousness of the consciousness of that object. This is already a reversal that is very difficult for the ordinary consciousness to grasp, since it must specifically renounce its ordinary nature. This is the mental operation that phenomenology accomplishes for philosophy, and it is why phenomenology already carries in itself a kind of initiation. The initiative is so difficult that we see, in our day, the title of "phenomenology" used in good faith by authors even when they are far from it, or in programs that are *toto caelo* distant. In fact, the total inversion proposed to the natural consciousness is best expressed in an Image that is really striking to see appear in Indian philosophy (in the Katha Upanishad) and in the *Ornement des Noces spirituelles* (Embellishment of spiritual marriage] of Ruysbroeck. It is the Image of a tree whose roots reach upward while its crown grows downward.†

Psychic here refers not to the paranormal but instead means "of or relating to the psyche." —*Trans.*

†Jung's foreword to *Introduction to Zen Buddhism*, xvi; *Gesammelte Werke,* vol. 11, § 890. See also J. van Ruysbroeck, *Œuvres choisies,* translated from the Middle Dutch and introduced by J. A. Bizet (Paris: Aubier, 1946), 228: "And he must climb up into the tree of belief, which grows downward, since it has its roots in the godhead."

There is more here than a phenomenology, since far from pro-
ceeding from a uniquely intellectual need, the "upsetting" questions
are rooted in an exercise that, originally at least, is religious. Their
experimental phase reveals the effort of man to free himself from the
egoified form (*Ichhaftigkeit*) of consciousness and to attain the reality of the inner man by discovering what makes and conditions the
essence of consciousness. From then on, outer things and consciousness no longer confront each other like two greatnesses each enclosed
in their own parentheses. The "empty" consciousness in Buddhist
terminology, being of spiritual poverty according to Meister Eckhart,
remains open to the action of an activity that is other, no longer felt
to be egoifying, but as the action of the non-I that has consciousness
as its object. It's as if the original "I" had emigrated and found itself
taken over by another subject taking the place of the "I."* "My soul is
infinite, I have swallowed the universe," the Zen monk can say. But
where and when is that heard? Only at "the point where the white
cloud seems to emerge from the mountain and immediately disappear." The essential has perhaps been said, for if this state corresponds
to what Baader was pointing to with his unique word *Cogitor,* which
overturns all Cartesian views, before intuition sets itself up permanently there will be a succession (a torrent) of discontinuous moments,
fleeting as lightning. From one moment to the next, the way is nevertheless delineated, and it is the way that we will continue to follow
step-by-step with our pondering of Jung's Buddhist studies.

From this point onward, the foreword to Suzuki's book provides
us with other essential indicators of consciousness that have undergone this metamorphosis. Here too, let us free ourselves from the
rational objection that consists in saying: "In itself consciousness has

---

*Jung's foreword to *Introduction to Zen Buddhism,* xvii: "O Lord . . . Instruct me in the
doctrine of the non-ego," quoted from the Laṅkāvatāra Sūtra in Suzuki, *Essays in Zen
Buddhism* (Boston: Beacon Press, 1952), 76; *Gesammelte Werke,* vol. 11, § 890, no. 28.

not changed, it is seeing with the same 'eyes' but is looking at a different object." Such an objection is an arbitrary and commonplace
interpretation taking no account of the new dimension that the new
spiritual state is witness to. It's not a question of seeing something
else but of seeing differently. When the Zen master questions, "Do
you hear the murmur of the brook? That is the entryway," it is very
clear that the hearing that he is calling for is quite other than hearing through the perceptive faculties—a transmutation of perception
and of objects is assumed. And that means already having overcome
the rational intellect, having made one's way to the Knowledge of the
Knower. It is a process of transformation (Wandlung), the carrying
out of which would be an insurmountable task for the pure, philosophical intellect. It is an exchange and a transformation of energies
of the soul that Jungian psychology can analyze and in doing so can
respond to the questions, "Is the application of such a process to a
Western consciousness conceivable? Is it desirable? And in what way?"

Our modern philosophical situation knows of no connection that
resembles the connection between the ancient philosophers and the
mystery religions. On their own, Faust or Zarathustra do not present
a single philosophy but something much more than that. Through a
process of dramatic transformation, they propose not a single thought,
but the "thinker of this thought," and that through this action there
must appear a radically transformed being "who not only looks upon
a new heaven and a new earth, but has created them."* In Christian
terms, that would be called a "conversion," and satori would correspond to an experience of religious conversion—we need still to specify the typology of that. In any case, it is in sharp contrast to the type
of experience that a method such as the *Spiritual Exercises* of Saint

---

*Jung's foreword to *Introduction to Zen Buddhism*, xii; *Gesammelte Werke*, vol. 11,
§ 892.

Ignatius of Loyola tends to promote. The frequency of the allusions that Jung makes to this method is remarkable, since it marshals all the resources of the person's imaginative powers. Regarding Jung's interest, we detect here something of a double factor: there is a sense of the affinity with psychotherapy that specifically calls upon all the energies of Active Imagination, and there is the contrast that is felt with the Zen Buddhist method, which demands the emptying from the consciousness of all prior representations. Already in the history of Christian spirituality, the Ignatian method offers the extreme originality of a restoration of Images, in perfect contrast to the poverty of Meister Eckhart or the spiritual spareness of Saint John of the Cross.

However, in spite of the nominal affinity between these two techniques (Ignatian and Jungian) in appealing to Active Imagination, I believe it is urgent to specify the difference, which is a measure of the affinity of Active Imagination with the Zen process—the paradox is an apparent one only.

Here is what we have: Loyola's Exercises tend to produce the intense imaginative representation of scenes reproducing or anticipating events of a real, sacred history. The scenes impose a frame and predetermine the form and the outcome of the spiritual experience. There is a presupposition, the preponderant role of which contrasts with the void, the state of emptiness, which, by the way, is prescribed precisely to eliminate all presupposition. As well, the analogies of satori that can be identified in some of the Christian mystics tend always to express themselves in paradoxical formulations having already surpassed the limits of heterodoxy. One cannot even conceive of the possibility of bringing together the contemplation of a text such as the sermon of Meister Eckhart mentioned above or of the paradoxes such as "God is a Name," with a contemplation of the Passion of the Savior delineated by the Exercises. In this type of experience or conversation, predetermined in this way by a collection of presuppositions, Jung certainly brings in the case of conversations arising in Protestantism (by faith, by prayer, by experience of the community). There will be an occasion to mention further along that Buddhist meditation, in the example chosen from the Pure Land sect, also provides the person meditating with presuppositions that lead him to an opening. Only here, it already is no longer a question reactivating imaginatively the real events of a sacred history but of conducting with Active Imagination a transmutation in symbols of perceptible data borrowed from the "real." However, it is clearly the Zen spiritual practice that offers the most perfect contrast. But wouldn't there then be this paradox: Zen discarding all Images and Jungian therapy bringing to bear all the resources of the Active Imagination? I think that we have here one of the most essential points in which our commentary might *(xxxx)*.

To resolve this paradox, we must begin from the essential character that Jung is pleased to point out in Zen Buddhism—its extreme individualism. It is present to such an extent that if the Buddhism of the Great Vehicle were to form something that resembled what we mean by a church, the Zen sect would then be an unbearable burden for it. (Because the paradoxical aspect in Zen Buddhism is that it is specifically there to provoke and welcome the experience of the "great liberation," which can only be a horror for any church institution as we think of them. Such an institution could not survive it.) Satori is an absolutely intimate experience, the most individual of all—to such an extent that neither the secret of the way that leads to it nor the form that it takes are communicable.* And there is exactly a necessary connection between the radically individual configuration of the method and the imperative that demands

---

*Jung's foreword to *Introduction to Zen Buddhism*, xix; *Gesammelte Werke*, vol. 11, § 894, no. 33.

an emptying out so as to liberate the consciousness from all preexisting images and from all originally conditioned representations; in short, from all received presuppositions. Whereas the final result of the Exercises, for example, is foreseen and expected, the koans* are so numerous that it is impossible to foresee the solutions, even when they are suggested. It is impossible to recognize, without objection, the rational connection with the data. In any case, no connection binds beforehand the liberty of the person meditating. The final result proceeds from nothing else but the most individual disposition of the adept. Because the emptiness produced by the elimination of all rational and conscious presuppositions leaves the depths free, or rather bottomless (Abgrund). From these depths, there will arise the absolutely individual, unforeseeable responses, meaning that the unconscious presuppositions are by definition neither abolished nor able to be abolished. They form the basic, present, and unconscious psychological disposition, which is whatever it may be, but it is not an emptiness and an absence of presuppositions. It is a factor given with and through Nature itself, and when Nature responds—and the experience of satori is such a response—it is the response of the deep nature of the adept, the nature that escapes the sway of Consciousness or whatever name one might give it: transconsciousness, supraconsciousness, or unconsciousness.† So that we can grasp the full import of the precept: "Look at the face you had

---

*"By *koan* is understood a paradoxical question, expression or action of the master. According to Suzuki's description it seems to be chiefly a matter of master questions handed down in the form of anecdotes. These are submitted by the teacher to the student for meditation. A classic example is the Wu- or Mu-anecdote. A monk once asked the master, 'Has a dog Buddha nature, too?' whereupon the master answered, 'Wu.' As Suzuki remarks, this 'Wu' means quite simply 'Wu,' obviously just what the dog himself would have said in answer to the question." From Jung's foreword to *Introduction to Zen Buddhism,* xix–xx; *Gesammelte Werke,* vol. 11, § 894, no. 33.

†Jung's foreword to *Introduction to Zen Buddhism; Gesammelte Werke,* vol. 11, § 898.

before your birth," because doing that is to deeply inspect what is absolutely one's own nature, and it is one's own nature that is, in Zen terms, the Buddha.

Thus, the radical absence of presuppositions that characterizes Zen in contrast to all other philosophical or religious meditation seems clearly to consist in this: that nothing else must be found there other than what, precisely, is to be found there—that is, man with all his nonconscious, spiritual presuppositions from which he can never separate himself, since they are not conscious! The response that seems to come from the void, the light that springs forth from deepest night, is always experienced as a marvelous and beauteous enlightenment.

From the process understood in this way, an initial difficulty is resolved, one that never fails to torment the rational, Western intellect engaging in a more or less profound reading of Buddhist texts. It is the affirmation of this void (śūnya) constantly repeated in the Great Vehicle and going hand in hand with the flowering of a metaphysical Imagination that develops a dizzying multitude of Buddhas, Bodhisattvas, Pure Lands, *aradis,* and so on. It really seems that if imposed Imaginings are what do away with the Buddhist void—for example, within the framework of the Ignatian Exercises, meaning that they are provided immediately to the state of conscious information and make the result predictable—then, in contrast to that, the experience of the abyss (*ab imo*), an experience that this emptiness itself permits for the individual meditator, and that produces a transmutation of modes and objects of perception. Such an experience liberates from these depths the wellspring that produces symbols. In other words, what is being basically contrasted is, on the one hand, the predictable program that leaves the imagination subsisting in its state of copies of what is perceived and, on the other hand, the natural and spontaneous production of symbols, operating, through the newly blossoming consciousness, as a transmutation of the perceived data that it turns into symbols. It is up to each individual consciousness to develop its own symbol or symbols, its own symbolic universe. At the same time, the paradox that we were pointing out above also becomes resolved. In Jungian therapy, the bringing to bear of Active Imagination tends not to impose a previously established repertoire of images but instead allows the most intimate and innermost recesses of the soul to be freed through the configuration of the soul's own symbols. And on this point, the affinity of the Active Imagination with the individualism of Zen Buddhism is affirmed through the positioning of this spontaneous production of symbolic images within what is targeted at the highest level and further is designated as a process of individuation that consists of becoming a total being.

This is also why the Zen spiritual experience offers a particularly propitious field of application to the Jungian studies of the soul's energetics. Given that consciousness is always partial and unilateral, given that it is only the subliminal or the whole unconscious region that furnishes a totality, and although it is never apperceptible as such, it is nonetheless like a virtual intuition of the whole. When the consciousness is emptied as much as possible of its contents, these contents fall, fleetingly, into the Unconscious. In the case of Zen, the energy captured in the contents of the consciousness is transferred either onto a representation of the void, or onto a koan. The energy reserves garnered in this way reinforce the charge of the unconscious up to a certain maximum, and through that, there increases in the same measure the ability of the unconscious to break through into consciousness. Of course, long training is needed to produce the maximum tension needed for this breaking through to occur. There is never anything arbitrary about that. It's a specific relationship, a connection of compensation regulating this emergence of unconscious content. What it brings necessarily completes and perfects the totality of the conscious orientation. In this way, a form of psychic existence is born that corresponds solely to this All that forms the individual person while eliminating the conflicts that tear the person apart.* Of course, this psychotherapy intends to eliminate the prejudice according to which the Unconscious harbors only infantile or morally inferior content. Specifically, another of Jung's essays shows us where the hermeneutic of Freud is situated in the light of Buddhist experience. Far from that, the Unconscious is "the matrix of all metaphysical assertions, of all mythology, all philosophy . . . and all forms of life which are based upon psychological suppositions."† In this same measure, all breaking through from the Unconscious is a response to a given situation in the Consciousness. This response arises from the ensemble of the possibilities of representation based in fact. That is, it arises from the overall arrangement that constitutes an overall Image of psychic existence in a state of simultaneity that is at least virtual.

These last indications allow us to envision the extreme care that Jung tries to inculcate in the reader seeking Knowledge as to which application of Zen is conceivable for Western man. First of all there is this: models are lacking. The spiritual history of the West offers nothing similar to the Zen masters, nor in general to anything similar to the role played by that great human figure, "the master," in Eastern spirituality. And are we then to picture many Westerners spending several years absorbed in resolving the paradox of a koan, or assuming the authority that a "conversion" confers on a Zen master when that conversion is just as much individually experienced as it is perfectly heterodox? It is because we lack these premises that most often such "authorities" degenerate into pathological cases.

---

*Jung's foreword to *Introduction to Zen Buddhism,* xxii; *Gesammelte Werke,* vol. 11, § 899.

†Jung's foreword to *Introduction to Zen Buddhism,* xxiii; *Gesammelte Werke,* vol. 11, § 899.

That there is no lack of more or less faithful disciples makes them no less suspect.

Perhaps then the text that we quoted here at the very beginning, taken from the introduction that we have just commented on, might indicate a more precise direction. Jungian psychotherapy is a dialectic relationship between doctor and patient,* a meeting of two totalities, two psychic collectives, for which all scholarly knowledge is only an instrument. The great work is metamorphosis (Wandlung), "conversion," but where it is a question of converting oneself to one's Self, which is perhaps the most difficult of conversions, because nothing in that is predetermined in advance, everything is indeterminate and indeterminable. The only criterion there is—as in Buddhism—is the falling away, the disappearance of the egoifying and egoified "I" (Ichhaftigkeit). The traditional atmosphere, the ground of the spiritual culture of Buddhism that Zen presupposes, has nothing identical to it in the West, in our culture, but it does have its counterpart. What corresponds to it is the whole of our spiritual culture that intends us necessarily to produce a conscious "I," a conscious understanding before dreaming of abolishing the egoified "I." We might think then that this dialectic relationship can be put in place with a book—on condition that one knows how to read and confront a book in the same way one knows how to read and confront a soul. And so we learn to turn our gaze inside to find the "I" we are searching for outside.† The rediscovered intellect might fall into the torments of demonic birth (Geburt), wander in mazes, be threatened with illusion, and worst of all: the silent solitude of the void in a time that it calls its own.‡

---

*Jung's foreword to *Introduction to Zen Buddhism*, xxv; *Gesammelte Werke*, vol. 11, § 904.

†Jung's foreword to *Introduction to Zen Buddhism*, xxvi; *Gesammelte Werke*, vol. 11, § 905.

‡Jung's foreword to *Introduction to Zen Buddhism*, xxvi; *Gesammelte Werke*, vol. 11, § 905.

To find an Eastern parallel to the torments and catastrophes that threaten the Westerner on his initiatory journey into total being, we must read the *Bardo Thödol* backward. We will be doing that further along, accompanied by Jung, who invites us to do just that, and we will be led to discover for ourselves the most personal response that C. G. Jung himself gave to this situation of consciousness, to the form of psychic existence of Western man in our times. Another lesson is going to bring us closer still to this response. Happily, Zen does not exert the same attractiveness as does the technique of hatha yoga, for example, for the European in need of physiological thought. The way of meditation that engenders the "spiritual body" is something else entirely. Pure Land meditation is one of the famous examples of yoga bringing to bear exercises that are purely of the mind. It is an example with which we feel infinitely more at ease than being faced with gymnastics or physiological practices aberrant to us. The amplification of symbols transmitted by *The Secret of the Golden Flower* will reveal to us in the best possible way the spiritual process involved in Jung's therapy of the soul. At the same time this process will be a direct response to the question, "What is the meaning of all that for us?"

2

PURE LAND

On *La Psychologie de la méditation orientale* [The psychology of oriental meditation]

With C. G. Jung's essay on the psychology of Eastern meditation, we find ourselves again in the spiritual climate of Japan, where we experienced Zen. The text that is analyzed and expanded upon here belongs in fact to the basic sacred texts of Pure Land Buddhism, which enjoyed the height of its flowering mainly in two schools founded in the twelfth century and thirteenth century in Japan by, respectively, Hōnen [Hōnen-bō Genkū] (1133–1212), founder of the Jōdo-shū sect or Pure Land school, and by his disciple Shinran (1173–1263), founder of the "Essence of Pure Land" sect (Jōdo Shinshū).* But the origins go much further back. This Amida Buddha is one of five "meditation Buddhas" (Dhyani Buddhas) introduced by Mahāyāna Buddhism as a hypostasis (the term is approximate) of a pure, original Buddha (Adi-Buddha or Mahābuddha). It is not possible to say what reasons pro-

---

*Corbin's original text misspelled the names of Hōnen and Shinran and gave incorrect dates. These errors are corrected here. —*Trans.*

duced this metaphysical flowering. All that can be determined is that the movement seems to be associated with the expansion that carried Buddhism beyond the borders of India. More specifically, the name of the Buddha who conferred his name to this Japanese "Amidism" is Amitābha (infinite light), or Amitāyus (infinite duration) in the original Sanskrit. Occupying a fixed position in the mandalas, he reigns over the Western Paradise, his own Buddhist Land, a land of bliss, or *sukhāvatī*. His compassion opens the way for his faithful; that is, those in whom Faith—or his wish—gives rise to the actual wish to be reborn in this Land where "they move forward toward nirvana without abandoning ecstasy and beatitude."

The origin of the Pure Land sect (totally ignored by the Lesser Vehicle) poses one of the most obscure problems in the history of Mahāyāna Buddhism. An Iranianist can do nothing other than support the judgment that seeks factors for Pure Land's triumph in the propagation of Buddhism outside of India, largely in the intermediate region of Serindia,* where the Iranian influence was dominant. With two principal Bodhisattvas (these "Heroes of the Spirit of Awakening") helping him (Avalokiteśvara and Mahāsthāmaprāpta), Amida/Amitābha forms, in effect, a triad in which the dominant connotations are Infinite Duration, Infinite Light, and Victorious Strength. All of these representations are familiar to the Iranian religions: Infinite Time from Zurvanism; Infinite Light from Mazdeism (Zoroastrianism); and Mithra from Mithraism, who supports the evocation of Maitreya, who consoles the Buddha of future times, whose relationship with Amitābha is not a chance connection. Do we need to remind readers of the well-known fact that the first translators (from Sanskrit into Chinese) of the Mahāyāna texts of the second century were the Arsacids, the Parthians, and

---

*Serindia refers to Chinese Central Asia. —*Trans.*

the Sogdians and that the Kushan Empire was as much Mazdean as it was Buddhist? However, it seems that "historical" exposition is really a hopeless endeavor, since the "material" traces have been very thoroughly worn away. Wouldn't disagreements founded on purely historical causality be no longer convincing? That is, those who believe they've shown that a given number of factors are sufficient to produce such and such a result—as if personal existence did not create an absolutely irreducible actual fact. Perhaps there is another way through which affinities that come to light might be valorized positively. For example, on the one hand, the dominant Mazdean concepts of the Fravartis incarnating voluntarily in the Saoshyant and, on the other hand, images of the Buddha in Pure Land Buddhism. The figures of Amahraspand and Izad of Mazdeism have more than once been compared with the angels and archangels of the Judeo-Christian tradition. The task certainly is not in vain. But if, alternatively, the Bodhisattvas are similarly proposed as the "angels" of Mahāyāna Buddhism, these figures may indeed have even more affinity with what are truly the "angels and archangels" of Mazdeism as they relate to the human condition, to its raison d'être, and to its perspectives. The role of Manichaeism cannot be forgotten here. But it is certainly not through the path of historicism that the problem of these relationships is going to be thought out. It is stunning how the metamorphosis of divine figures is most often treated the same way as one would treat changes in identity papers, or even window display items that from time to time are sent back to the factory to be upgraded. Of what does the essential spiritual reality of these figures consist—the untrammeled reality? The terms of the problem are not understandable or resolvable except through meditation. And it is specifically the "meditations" of Jung that we are commenting on here that provide an example that shows us the way, and this is why the problem, of which Pure Land Buddhism is an exemplary case, should be raised. Doing so is to create a "fact" that our science of religions will instinctively find "dangerous." But that science has other dangers it should heed, such as crumbling under the weight of an increasing eruption that has no other meaning than to feed sterile polemics, unable as it is to respond to the silent expectation that has been entrusted to it. Or the danger of finding itself ceding the way to bubbly improvisations by amateurs.

The spiritual origins of Amidism are linked to the form of spiritual existence that the term *bhakti* (devotion, love) evokes. During the time of a Buddha, before the Buddha that we regard as the "historical Buddha," Amida was still only the Bodhisattva Dharmakara. He took the vow not to receive the correct-complete Awakening, to refuse the supreme state of nirvana "until in the ten directions there are still beings believing in me and loving me heart and soul while wishing to be reborn in my kingdom and not having been able to do so." This vow defines perfectly the essence of a Bodhisattva as the ideal being of Mahāyāna Buddhism. The sects of Pure Land Buddhism experience Amida's relationship with beings as an infinite love, forever without wrath or anger, and wishing to save them from suffering and ignorance. It is this salvation of human beings through pure compassion and the grace of love that gave rise to the sense of an affinity with the doctrine of salvation through grace and pure goodness in Luther. Rudolph Otto reported a moving testimony of this. If a man thinks with all his strength, right to the very limits of his spiritual force, of Amida's Western Paradise, and experiences, in listening to the *sūtras,* absolute faith in Amida's vow as he forms in himself the vow to be reborn there, he is already assured that after death he will be reborn in this Pure Land. The means offered to the faithful for this spiritual connection flowering in an outpouring of faith and love are basically conditioned by the doctrine that "the Bodhisattva who, on hearing the name of Amitābha, desires to see him, can see him by thinking constantly of

the region where he is."* In broad outline and without referring here
to how the two aspects of the method were able to be combined or to
have one supplant the other, this "thinking of the Buddha" was able
to be merged with "pronouncing the name" (*nomen est numen!*). This
then is the recitation of the name of Amida, a practice designated as
nembutsu (*namu Amida butsu,* adoration of the Buddha of Infinite
Light). Similarly, through the practice of a meditation of visualization,
as the mind is purified by this exercise, Amitābha Buddha is reflected
in it as in a mirror. The Buddha and the mind of the person meditating
become one. It is also true to say that, in this mirror, the mind is looking at itself, or the Buddha is looking at himself. For this meditation
of visualization, the basic texts of the Pure Land sect offer a support of
unlimited resources. First of all, the Sukhāvatīvyūha Sūtra, where the
statement of the forty-eight vows making up the great solemn vow of
Amitābha contains the description of the beauties of the Pure Land,
the splendor of the beings who are reborn there, the marvels of their
contemplations, and their demiurgic ecstasy. In addition, there is the
Amitāyurdhyāna Sūtra, or sūtra of the meditation of the Buddha of
Infinite Duration. This is a teaching given by Shakyamuni Buddha
to Queen Vaidehi and her five hundred attendants, inviting them to
practice sixteen forms of meditation on the Pure Land and on its lord,
the Buddha of the Setting Sun of Infinite Light. This is the sūtra that
forms the textbook of Jung's study of the philosophy of Eastern meditation. We need to provide a brief summary of its contents before pro-
ceeding to commentary and amplification.

Of the sixteen forms of meditation, the study only deals with a
few, the importance of which turn out to be basic to the practice of

---

*Carl Gustav Jung, "Zur Psychologie östlicher Meditation," in *Mitteilungen der
Schweizerischen Gesellschaft der Freunde ostasiatischer Kultur* 5 (1943): 227; *Gesammelte
Werke,* vol. 11, § 926. This text was reprinted in *Symbolik des Geistes: Studien über
psychische Phänomenologie,* edited by R. Schärf (Zürich: Rascher Verlag, 1948).

this yoga that allows one to be reborn in Amitābha's Paradise. To achieve this, it is necessary to produce a perception of the Western Paradise through concentrated thought: turning toward the west, ordering the thoughts through a meditation concentrated on the setting sun, fixing one's awareness and sight upon it, then closing the eyes while maintaining this clear and stable Image. This is the first meditation, a mental perception of the Sun. Next, one must produce a perception of Water: contemplating clear water while maintaining the Image unchanged. Then produce a perception of Ice, imagining it bright and transparent, then imagining an Apparition of lapis lazuli. "The ground is made up of lapis lazuli. In its diaphanous depths, you distinguish sharply the golden banner of the seven jewels, extending in the eight directions of the compass. On this ground of lapis lazuli, cables of gold are connected in crosses." Once this perception has been formed, you meditate on each of its constituent parts, one after the other, maintaining the images absolutely clearly, without wavering, eyes open or closed. You do this continuously, except during sleep. Whoever has achieved this state of perception, achieved the state of *samādhi* (concentration, introspection) is capable of seeing the Land of Happiness, the sukhavatī, clearly and distinctly. It is a state that cannot be completely explained. It is the third form of meditation. You must meditate on the tree of jewels of Amitābha's Land; in it you must "visualize" Water divided among seven lakes. In the middle of each lake are sixty million lotus flowers, each made up of seven jewels. All the flowers are perfectly round and of the same size. The water flowing among the flowers produces melodious sounds.

After this, you must practice the Amitābha meditation itself, forming the perception of a lotus flower on the ground of seven jewels. Each flower has eighty-four thousand petals, each petal as many veins, each vein has many branches, each one of which can be distinguished clearly. . . . After this you will be able to perceive the Buddha, because the body of each perfect Buddha is a Body of Essence (*dharmakāya*) so that he can penetrate into the consciousness of all beings. If you perceive the Buddha, your consciousness has the thirty-two signs of perfection that you see in the Buddha. Finally, it is your consciousness that becomes or, better still, is in fact Buddha. The ocean of true and universal knowledge of all Buddhas has its source in our own consciousness and thought. This is why you must direct your thought with undivided attention on a perfect medita-tion forming the perception of this perfect Buddha (Tathāgata)—the Arhat, the Saint, the Enlightened Perfected One. . . . If you have seen him sitting on the lotus, your spiritual vision will become clear, you will be able to see the beauty of this Buddha Land, and along with this Land you will see all the Buddhas of the ten universes. . . . From those who practice this meditation, it is said that they have seen the body of all the Buddhas, and that they have perceived also the Mind that is great compassion. . . . If you have attained this per-ception, you will form for yourself the Image of yourself as you will be born in the world of happiness, in the western region, seated with legs crossed on a lotus flower. This flower enfolds you within itself, and then it opens. When it spreads open, your body is surrounded by five hundred rays of clear light. Your eyes are open so that you can see the multitude of Buddhas and Bodhisattvas as they fill the whole sky. . . .

We have hugely condensed this text of fascinating images, but we could not be satisfied with a simple reference in order to appreciate the exe-gesis that, from one figure to the next, must lead us back to the central symbol, the one that, at the end of this outline, will be presented to us as a Diamond Body. Let us follow this progression in the company of Jung. The initial characteristic of the exercise is a concentration on the setting Sun. The Image can remain imprinted on the retina for a time once the eyes are closed, without there being, strictly speaking, any hypnosis: it is a question of a meditation, of a reflection, a "creation of the Sun" and its properties and meanings. It's a matter of making oneself translucent as if within an internal "sunning." As the circular figure playing a great role in the continuation of the meditations, the solar disc is presented as a model for the Images that the meditation has to produce next, shining as it does its light upon them in advance. The Water meditation that follows no longer draws its support from a sense perception but is produced by the Active Imagination from the reflective surface, mirroring perfectly the light of the sun. Then this same Active Imagination transforms this Water into a luminescent and diaphanous Ice. Here Jung's analysis uncovers a process in perfect correspondence with the phases of inner transmutation that allow us to identify the symbols of alchemical operation in the following phases. A first transmutation conducted by the organ of Meditation— that is, the Active Imagination—is that of the still immaterial Light of the Solar Image as the matter of Water, which is also in the subtle state. Finally this Water takes on the "material" stability of ice. The vision undergoes a concretization (*solve et coagula*), thanks to which the Imagined Creation solidifies, coagulates. From that point on, the Imagined Creation takes the place of Physical Nature. The world of perceptible matter from natural space is transmuted into a new reality. The naturally bluish tint of ice transmutes then into lapis lazuli, and with this ground of mineral consistency (certainly luminous and transparent, since it is from a subtle imaginative condition) a real, absolute foundation is created. Meditation, plunging into the transparency of the blue ground like a lake of glass, discerns flaming in the depths the banner of gold. From successive transmutations we then have the birth of symbol. The alchemy of meditation intensifies further the radiating energy of the initial Solar Image. The ogdoadic symbol shines like a thousand million suns, while the golden cables, extending their network on the "system," announce that stability is assured, that no foundering can threaten the imaginative process. The symbol with eight rays is already Amitābha's Pure Land. The water of its lakes with their admirable sonorities, corresponding here to the *Aqua permanens* of the alchemists, is the *Aqua Doctrina,* the pure doctrine of the Pure Land Buddha. And it is here in the heart that the imaginative epiphany of the Amitābha Buddha occurs, coinciding with the intention of the active mind of the meditator. That is to say, the soul that produces these images and these perceptions is Buddha himself. Or more precisely stated: the figure of Amitābha Buddha seated in the heart of a lotus in the center of his octagonal Land. The Buddha, whose great compassion welcomes all beings, therefore the meditator as well, is outlined, is put forward in the vision, and appears as the authentic Self of the meditator, liberated at the end of a long exercise of spiritual reconstruction from the egoified and egoifying form of the "I" that blinds, separates, and isolates the Self in the illusory antimonies of being and nonbeing.

Thus we see that the symbol of the Pure Land is an excellent example of the "unifying symbols" that appear only when one arrives at the culmination of the path of individuation—a culmination that is close to the Buddhist teaching and that ought to no longer ring like a paradox, since we know that this individuation, a culmination of the transmutation of the psyche in the way that Jung's psychology brings it to bear—specifically means liberation from the egoifying consciousness. This is the equilibrium that comes into play between the Self and the Unconscious when the inner psyche "has been experienced as being just as real, as effective, and as psychologically true as the world of external reality." *(Compare this with Tucci.)* Then there appear "these symbols," which reproduce the *imago* of the totality of the psyche—in this case, the mandala of the Pure Land at the center of which is visualized the figure of Amida Buddha as the central and unifying symbol of the Self.

Here too, as in each of these Jungian Buddhist exercises, the question arises: What does all this mean for us from the point of view of practical spiritual effectiveness? Of course, the caution must be repeated: we are not dealing here with childish imagination, or even some "monkey business," which would simply be an excuse for diversifying unconscious projections. However, if the yoga of Pure Land Buddhism seems to us to be closer than any other, and if it suits us to speak of it with a respect that our own rationalism has not always observed, alas, with regard to our own Christian *mysterium fidei,* it would be entirely inadequate to limit ourselves to saying that its present relevance would be, first and foremost, a documentary and comparative one—our pretext for such a limitation being that in general the forms and figures of Buddhism have been determined by quite other conditions than our own in the history of the spirit. Doing so would be pure historicism, the worst egoifying form of scholarly awareness, amounting to distancing oneself from the responsibilities of one's own presence by projecting oneself into a fictitious objectivity. We have been trying in what has already been said to delineate the connection that underlies both the resemblance and the contrast between the constitutive process of the Jungian therapy of the soul on the one hand and the initiations practiced in traditional cultures on the other hand. The contrast consists essentially in this: the traditional cultures are characterized by the observance of rites and symbols determined and imposed by a Tradition, whereas psychotherapy aims basically to provoke a natural and spontaneous production of symbols. In short, traditional initiations tend to provoke, in the far recesses of the soul and of consciousness, the blossoming of an Image and a conception that they themselves are part of, to which they themselves belong, and which they themselves represent. In contrast, if the Jungian process of individuation tends toward a spiritual, ethical, and religious integration, the program of which is not fixed in advance but is conditioned by the spontaneous learning and research of each individual; and if, consequently, the form in which the individual's conception of the world, his "unifying symbol" will blossom, is well and truly the fruit and result of his own experience—and not the content proposed in the course of his "preparation"—then we can glimpse what relevance there might be in questioning the meaning of a possible integration, diversified according to each case, of the highly evolved doctrines and spiritual practices of Buddhism.

This is why the rapprochement already outlined by Jung between the meditation of Pure Land Buddhism and the spiritual method of the Exercises of Saint Ignatius of Loyola* is eminently instructive. Their underlying similarity is based on the fact that both of them, unlike Zen, propose a schema for the awakening of the mind that establishes ahead of time the formulations, the path to be followed, and how long it will take. We believe however that it is necessary to bring out a highly significant structural difference between the two. In broad outline, we find, on the one hand, a method tending to a reproduction in the mind of perceptible data relating to events of a sacred history, past or future, whereas on the other hand we have a transmutation conducted by an alchemical Meditation, which transforms all perceptible data into symbols, amounting to the ontological establishment of the intermediary world of the Imagined. In this latter case, the production of symbols literally accomplishes a transmutation of the psyche. The mental iconography, which is the receptacle and the support of this process, is the sign, the announcement of this transmutation. The meditator is progressively transferred from the foreground of a visible phenomenon to a background—that

---

*"Zur Psychologie östlicher Meditation," 232; *Gesammelte Werke*, vol. 11, § 937.

is, to the spiritual direction of the meditations.* He is also transferred to the sphere of the psyche where Sun and Water are stripped
of their physical objectivity and become the symbols of content in
the psyche. The meditation amounts to a descent to a source in the
psyche, toward the Unconscious itself, from the depths of which
Sun and Water have emerged, from among a multitude of possible
symbolic images, precisely without there being anything arbitrary as
such in their spontaneity. With the lapis-lazuli ground, the meditator has, in a certain way, created for his vision a "solid body," thanks
to which the figures of his inner world assume a concrete reality that
takes the place of the external world. In the gold standard contemplated through the transparency of this ground of mystic mineral, in
a way he sees a figure of the Source of consciousness, formerly invisible and without form—incapable of form. For Dhyāna (meditation,
ecstasy) as a descent into the depths of the Unconscious, this standard takes on a form and a figure. Similar to the transfer of spiritual energy already observed with Zen, everything takes place here
as if the Light of consciousness that had ceased to illuminate objects
in the perceptible external world, revealed little by little the darkness of the Unexplored, from which there arises then the primordial
Image—Buddha Amitābha as imago of the totality of the psyche.

We have just raised an initial difference—regardless of the
similarities—between Pure Land yoga and the Ignatian Exercises.
There is another highly interesting difference. No doubt the two
methods share the common trait of seeking success by prescribing for
the meditator the object of his contemplation, by indicating to him
the Image on which he is to be concentrating. In so doing, each of
them are concerned to eliminate "fantasies" of no value, the wandering
and the mayhem that the collapse of a poorly regulated mental schema

---

*"Zur Psychologie östlicher Meditation," 232; *Gesammelte Werke,* vol. 11, § 935.

provokes, but even there the difference comes to light. Of course, we don't want to stop here at the often violent criticisms from inside and outside the Church of Rome that have been formulated against the Ignatian Exercises. Most often these criticisms proceed from a haughty prejudice, from an intellectual disdain for the Image and the reality of Images, the valorization of which is precisely an originality in the history of Christian spirituality. But it is still the case that the directed practice of the Exercises takes place in the spiritual and institutional framework of the Church of Rome. It is not our business to judge its success or its failure. We simply want to observe that, even if the yoga of Amida Buddha prescribes a meditation schema, the Pure Land Buddhist sect is far from offering a "framework" similar to that offered by the church in the Western sense. And there is more. The peril, the presentiment of which inspires a meditation schema that is ignored by Zen, for example—this peril turns out to be quite different in the two cases. We have noted that the guiding text of Pure Land Buddhism does not envision failure or collapse, and this lack of foresight highlights a structural difference in the zones of the psyche that must be passed through. Jung analyzes this difference with an admirable discernment.*

The "danger zone" to be traversed is that which, in Jungian terminology, is designated as the Personal Unconscious. This is the zone of shadows that harbors everything one would like not to admit, everything one would prefer to forget, repressed memories, everything "that is thought and felt in a subliminal way," and projected on others—since it is so much more comfortable to preach to others about what they should be or do, instead of beginning the improvement of the whole through an improvement of oneself. The zone of shadows that

---

*"Zur Psychologie östlicher Meditation," 233–34; *Gesammelte Werke*, vol. 11, § 938–40.

one must traverse and move through, with the risk of never attaining a trace of what this yoga promises, includes the preconscious as well as the subconscious—these border zones of Freudian dogma for which the *Bardo Thödol* will be able to define the function in our study below. Buddhist meditation shows us both how the problem of its integration does not arise for us in terms of Freudian psychoanalysis and how, when addressed in fact thanks to the Jungian psychology of the Unconscious, it justifies also all the warnings against total, uncritical acceptance of yoga by a European.

About this zone of shadows, it must be said that Buddhist meditation considers that, to all intents and purposes, it has already been crossed. This is why it does not foresee any mayhem or collapse among the wandering "fantasies," which of course have nothing to do with an Active Imagination capable of transmuting, or giving a real psychic substance to the visions. Certainly, Buddhist experience is well acquainted with the world of *kleshas* (passions), but it is not familiar with the moral conflict that world implies for us—the "ethical dilemma that separates us from our shadow"—the mind's Knowledge in opposition to Nature. That is why the lapis-lazuli ground remains opaque to us, since we first must respond to the question of Evil in Nature and in the "natural" world.* Conversely, when interpreted in terms of Jungian psychology, Pure Land yoga can show us what it has come to.

Let us follow this interpretation closely. Because the Contemplation Sūtra of the Amitāyus Buddha presupposes that zone of shadows of our personal "fantasies"—that is, the personal unconscious—has been crossed, this sūtra progresses by arousing symbolic figures that, at first glance, can seem strange to us: a radiating geometric figure, an ogdoad, and at its heart a lotus on which a Buddha is seated. The

---

*"Zur Psychologie östlicher Meditation," 234; *Gesammelte Werke,* vol. 11, § 942.

decisive experience is finally when the meditator recognizes that he is himself Buddha. The knot of destiny that was tied by his "story" and that provided his framework is untied by this recognition. The symbol of a concentric structure does not appear to the vision in the mind until the concentration in the mind has let go of all impressions from the world of the senses. This is the prerequisite alchemy. The world of the consciousness that latches on to objects, to representations of external objects—this world disappears, and then there arises from the lapis lazuli depths a bursting forth of the elaboration of the world of Amitābha. Psychologically, this means that, behind or underneath the world of instincts and personal "fantasies," there exists a deeper layer of the Unconscious. In contrast to the chaotic disorder of the kleshas, it is characterized by supreme harmony and order. To the chaotic multitude of the kleshas, this layer of the Unconscious opposes the all-inclusive unity of the bodhimaṇḍala, the magic and enchanted circle of Awakening or Enlightenment. The suprapersonal Unconscious, embracing the psycho-cosmic whole, appears only through the diaphanous ground of lapis lazuli—that is, when the personal unconscious has become transparent, since the personal unconscious is a simple, superficial layer resting on the foundation of the collective unconscious. All the power and extreme fertility of Jungian analysis is evident here in this integration undertaken as a meditation on Buddhist meditation, justifying in a new light the demand for a unique role that we have read about earlier in the essay on Zen. We know that in this active concept of Jung's psychological phenomenology the word *collective* has sometimes created misunderstandings. This word is being used to designate a general structure of the psyche, a universal morphology of the psyche, just as there is a common morphology of the human body. We would have preferred the simpler transconsciousness, but so be it. It remains that "it is the primordial Datum from which the concept ceaselessly arises," "the prodigious spiritual heritage of the evolution of the species that is reborn, that returns in each individual structure." We have here one of the notions that most radically differentiates the complex psychology of Jung from the psychology of Freud as seen in what the two offer and in their results. The Images of this deeper Unconscious are of mythological character. They are suprapersonal and common in their strength for all human beings. In form and content, they are in harmony with the primordial representations that are at the base of mythologies. And this is why our Western psychology measures up to yoga in the sense that it is capable of demonstrating scientifically the existence of a unifying foundational layer of the Unconscious. It is not surprising that, being struck by this remarkable correspondence, Jung chose the Sanskrit term *mandala* to designate the concentric order in which the mythological motifs are arranged and whose presence were deciphered by him in the suprapersonal Unconscious. The field of investigation is immense, since each *imago mundi* provides a theme.* Christian iconography offers multiple examples in psycho-spiritual realities that are much less "something to be explained" than "something that explains." I mean those recurrences in the face of which the historical explanation is at a loss, since it is looking superficially for a causal connection (in line of descent or influence, and so on), in which the *(XXXX)* will never be found.

This essay on Pure Land Buddhism is ending with a slow adagio that seems to be drowning in a silence where a heavy question threatens. If we omit the exceptional cases of the mystical paradoxes of a Meister Eckhart, of an Angelus Silesius, and a few others, it is still the case that between the Christian mandala and the Buddhist mandala

---

*That is, by way of history; for example, if we look for the introspective value of the medieval philosophy of Nature, we see that it always moves in a circle. (Carl Gustav Jung, "Zur Psychologie östlicher Meditation," 235; *Gesammelte Werke,* vol. 11, § 944.) Which is why on this experimental psychology path we have cases of the recurrence of the mandala.

there remains a subtle and enormous difference. In his meditation, the Buddhist experiences his identifying with, his merging with, the Buddha *(compare the theopathic locutions of Sufism: Bastami—Ruzbehan Baqli—the collection of Dara Shikuh):* certainly our own philosophical categories have been and are able to lead us into many misunderstandings about the conditions and the meaning of this merging. (Since we always position ourselves in front of alternatives, impelled to decide among monotheism, polytheism, or pantheism! But we won't discuss that here.) It remains the case that the spiritual experience of the Christian tends to be expressed not in forms such as "I am Christ," but in harmony with the Pauline formulation, "It is Christ that lives in me" [Galatians 2:20]. The Christian comes from the world of perishable, ephemeral, and egoifying consciousness; the Buddhist always rests on the eternal foundation of the inner Nature that is in a state of union with the divinity.* This contrast poses in itself something like a silent question. (The possible integration beyond any sterile dogmatic confrontation?)

In the end, Jung's commentary on the *Bardo Thödol* will provide us with an allusion, the sense and amplification of which will be discovered at the end of the essay on *The Secret of the Golden Flower* when we will be led to the most personal response given elsewhere by Jung.

---

*"Zur Psychologie östlicher Meditation," 237; *Gesammelte Werke,* vol. 11, § 949.

3

THE TIBETAN
BOOK OF THE DEAD
On the *Bardo Thödol*

Everything said up to this point shows us how Jungian psychology places high value on fundamental Buddhist intuition, which our rational philosophy confronts as a paradox painful to the point of hallucination, or which our historical criticism considers and then relegates to the position of an imposing but strange and exotic curiosity. This valorization has been made on the basis of a psychic reality recognized not only in its own autonomy and specificity but also in its primacy, in the sense that if, instead of accepting unconditionally what we call the "data" (all the constitutive data of our knowledge and our sciences, in short, all the data of our life), we ask ourselves the question, "Who is then the Giver of these data?" the secret of the answer is in this primacy of the soul.

(Remember the reservations already stated on the use of this word. We do not mean to affirm XXXX in any way against the Buddhist negations— ref. perhaps Suzuki, in the Honolulu volume. Dayol already does this above.)

No doubt one might say that our systems of idealist philosophy—

for example, that of Fichte—have stated something like that. Of course. Also we have no lack of remarkable studies on the philosophical idealism of Buddhism. However, just the examples of Zen and the yoga of Pure Land Buddhism in themselves are enough to suggest that they move on a plane of mental accomplishment soaring above the perspectives of idealist philosophy alone; just as the path of individuation that the therapy of the soul engages in also goes beyond the program of a simple philosophy, even were it to be an existential one. If we now attempt to draw together all the results of the psychological commentary written by Jung for the German translation of the Tibetan Book of the Dead, the *Bardo Thödol,* it is not only because of the link that, in the person of the Bodhisattva Avalokiteśvara, connects the Tibetan Buddha to the Pure Land Buddha, but also because this extraordinary book pushes beyond the limit the Buddhist intention and its implications. By "beyond the limit," we mean beyond death and the present status of the human condition.

It is with extreme interest that we learn that, since its translation into a European language, this book has become what might be called C. G. Jung's bedside table book—his constant companion in fact. As every reader who has studied it knows, this book is not a funerary ritual. It is a teaching that is addressed to the dead person himself, beyond death, to guide him through the phenomena and the Apparitions whose metamorphosis he experiences in the course of his existence during the transition, or passage; that is to say, the existence on the intermediary plane of the *bardo*—an existence that extends over forty-nine symbolic days until his reincarnation either in the earthly world or in an intermediary paradise. Unlike the Egyptian Book of the Dead, about which, as Jung declares, one can only say either too much or too little, the philosophy that the *Bardo Thödol* implies or states is a philosophy conceivable in human terms. It speaks to the man, not to Gods or to someone primitive. And this philosophy is the quintessence of Buddhist psychological criticism. From the very beginning, then, we are faced with the initial situation that characterizes all fortuitous or unprepared encounters between Buddhism and the "enlightened" European. If the European begins to read, for example, that the peaceful and friendly deities, as well as the wrathful and threatening deities, are simply samsaric projections of the human soul, he will immediately declare himself to be either in perfect agreement (if he is a man of some feeling against religious "dogma"), or, on the contrary, he will proclaim that what we have here is a dangerous and inadmissible negation of metaphysical "truth." Unfortunately, something too obvious pushed the man in the first case into a perfect misunderstanding; his agreement is not an agreement at all. As for the man in the second case, the danger that he is denouncing is precisely the one that he himself is threatened by, and the one that Buddhist Awakening proposes be surmounted. Basically, both the first and the second are unable to realize that the manifested divinities are projections of the soul, without "objective" consistency, and at the same time they are unable to posit these projections as being, in themselves, perfectly "real." All the power of the Buddhist effort to go beyond the antinomies of our categories resides in such an example. In general the Westerner likes "clarity"—for example, "God is" or "God isn't." There is "I" and "non-I." And the idea that his overall psychic personality is "more than I" is already rather disturbing to him. He no longer feels "at home." And this is precisely why, upon hearing, for example, that the divinities are projections of the soul, it is immediately toward this little, empirical "I," delimited by the single horizon of his rational consciousness, that he brings this declaration, either for the precise reason of enjoying it (it is very flattering for the little imperialism of the "I"), or to be alarmed by it (through a misunderstood humility). One way or another, it is the same implicit meaning: the "soul" is something so small, so weak, so "subjective"—and against this subjectivity one makes appeal to the judgment of the Mind, because it goes without saying that, however subjective it might be, this judgment must be understood as judgment of the universal Mind, or even the absolute Mind.* It also goes without saying that a statement such as the following will remain perfectly unintelligible: "Recognize the Void in your own intelligence, recognize consciousness as Buddhahood and consider Buddhahood as your own consciousness: this is to dwell in the state of the divine Mind of the Buddha."

(For example, find in the Bardo Thödol—Evans-Wentz, p. 82.*)*

Nevertheless, such a saying tacitly states the presuppositions of Buddhist teaching. With regard to those presuppositions that we are focusing on here, we prefer to consider, on the one hand, that they share the antinomic character of all metaphysical statements. Otherwise we would be allowing ourselves to be imprisoned in some alternative, giving substance to another branching by way of thought (and thereby "emptying" both branches). On the other hand, there is the idea that there exists a qualitative difference among degrees of consciousness and that the metaphysical realities and statements are conditioned by them. This, consequently, we are saying, installs a solidarity between psychology and ontology. The planes of being are planes of meditation or ecstasy. The cosmology will be, insofar as it is psycho-cosmology, a cosmology of ecstasy. Already here we have the answer to the frequent reproach, "It's only psychology." Is that all psychology is then? And if that's all it is, then we have to agree that psychology, when that's *not* all it is, is to be found in the fact that the soul is the inner, divine creative power that makes metaphysical statements. It "posits" distinctions between metaphysical entities. It is not only the condition of this

---

*Carl Gustav Jung, "Commentaire psychologique du Bardo Thödol (*Das tibetanische Totenbuch*)," in *Psychologie et orientalisme* (Paris: Albin Michel, 1985), 169; *Gesammelte Werke,* vol. 11, § 835.

metaphysical kingdom, it is this kingdom itself.* What we have here is not a rational thesis to be debated along with other theses. This fact refers to a transcendent state in which it would be experienced and verified that the experience and the thing experienced are inseparably united—like the color yellow and the substance gold, like salt and the taste of salt.

Let us listen to the directives of the Bardo Thödol that the reader, at the moment of death, must recite into the ear of the dying person that he is assisting: "O nobly born, listen. Now thou art experiencing the Radiance of the Clear Light of Pure Reality . . . Thine own intellect, which is now voidness, yet not to be regarded as of the voidness of nothingness, but as being the intellect itself, unobstructed, shining, thrilling, and blissful is the very consciousness, the All-Good Buddha. Thine own consciousness, not formed into anything, in reality void, and the intellect, shining and blissful, these two, are inseparable. The union of them is the Dharma-Kāya [the Body of Essence] state of Perfect enlightenment. [The state of perfect enlightenment or the fundamental Clear Light mother and the Clear Light produced second. Their union takes place in the unified Clear Light.]† *(Y.T. p. 238 no. 163 and following pages see 12–13—E, 97, 238 in note, 241 no. 197, p. 244—compare same image Evans-Wentz p. 105; also, p. 81 no. 2 the "father" and the "mother" conjunction of the light that allows one to see and the light that is seen, recall the Mazdean, Daena. I am thyself. Evans-Wentz note p. 57—note the Apparition of the second Clear Light in the second stage of the Chikhai Bardo, Evans-Wentz p. 83.)*

---

*Jung, "Commentaire psychologique," 169; *Gesammelte Werke*, vol. 11, § 836.
†The text in square brackets is Corbin's interpolation, which he then expands upon in his aside. The page references in the aside seem to refer to the German edition of the Tibetan Book of the Dead. It is unclear what "Y.T." stands for at the beginning of the author's aside. —*Trans.*

Thine own consciousness, shining, void, and inseparable from the Great Body of Radiance, hath no birth, nor death, and is the Immutable Light—Buddha Amitābha."*

The immediate and definitive liberation from the circle of rebirth depends on the knowledge of this primordial Clear Light. He who, at the moment of his death, is capable of knowing his own essence, his consciousness laid bare just like the state of Clear Light, unites himself permanently with the dharmakāya. He is not required to know the trials of karmic illusions of the intermediate state of the bardo. But this realization is only possible as a result of a long spiritual training.

However, it is understandable that on first reading of this simple fragment, to say nothing of the whole book, there rings for the Western reader a dubious or even unbearable overtone. The faithful believer will be convinced in hearing this that "God is being taken away from him." Whereas, at the same time, the Eastern soul, knowing itself to be the light of divinity, recognizes that the divinity is the soul, and in so doing it has no need to affirm a "Supreme God," withstanding infinitely better its paradoxes than Angelus Silesius, for example, who manages to avoid the "cherubic voyager." In the end, almost all men would prefer to suffer the blows and oppression of external things, the multitude of data, rather than asking who has given them. Let us take note here of the expression in Avicennism: *Dator formarum*. This is exactly the question. To be precise, it is the angel who is none other than the Holy Spirit. A whole comparative study could be established from the point of view of (transcendental) psychology based on what is touched upon here. As Jung remarks, it seems that such a question has been asked only by a few thoughtful individuals who were trying to understand what they believed, people of an essentially gnostic tem-

---

*W. Y. Evans-Wentz, ed., *The Tibetan Book of the Dead, or, The After-Death Experiences on the Bardo Plane, According to Lama Kazi Dawa-Samdup's English Rendering*, 3rd ed. (Oxford/New York: Oxford University Press, 2000).

perament, believing in a Savior who would be called, like the Savior of the Mandeans, "Knowledge of Life" (Manda d'Hayyē).

In fact, to see how the world is "given" by the essence of the soul, there must be a great, inner overturning, the sacrifice of a total conversion. Otherwise, this simple proposition extended beyond the premises of the conversion can produce only an absurd and alarming sound, because the giver would be identified with the egoifying and egoified "I," so "full of himself" that all the imperialisms of his egoistic animal nature think that they are justified. This is why attempts of this kind were always the object of secret initiations that included a symbolic death announcing this total overturning. So—afterward, yes—no longer do I see how the world knocks me about, but how I make it.

The intent of the *Bardo Thödol* is precisely to have the dead person recall initiation experiences, the teaching of his spiritual master. All in all, it is an initiation of the dead person to the existence of the life of the bardo (literally, "between-two"), just as the initiation of the living person was (as in the mystery religions) a preparation for the beyond. For the living person, the initiation was first of all an overturning of his intimate sense, a psychological beyond, a separation from an inner state of darkness and unconsciousness—in short, a state of enlightenment and of triumph over the data. This initiatory character of the *Bardo Thödol* thus outlined, if we include this other remark* that, while being on the highest psychological plane, is still at the medical prepsychological stage—that is, at the stage in which only the statements are understood, explained, and criticized, while the Instance that produces these statements and judgments remains cleared of blame as if by virtue of a general convention. One sees, as soon as this question of the Instance is posed, the possibility of an

---

*Jung, "Commentaire psychologique," 68; *Gesammelte Werke,* vol. 11, § 834.

extraordinary overturning that will allow the *Bardo Thödol* to become in itself an initiation for those who are alive.* This is evidenced, let us not forget, in the prescription to read and to reread this book during one's life, "to restore the divinity of the soul that was lost in birth."†

This is why Jung's hermeneutics proposes that we read this text backward—in reverse order.

To understand this initially inoffensive proposition, one must have in mind the structure of the *Bardo Thödol*. Three main phases determine the major divisions of the book. There is the bardo at the moment of death (Chikhai Bardo), in which the Clear Light illuminates two possible aspects—primordial or secondary, Mother and Son. The recognition of this, as we have said, marks the definitive Deliverance. However, if the individual perceiving is not able to recognize it, the second bardo, called Chonyid Bardo, begins. It is a transitory state of the experience of reality in which the dead person awakens through a process similar to birth. One by one, he sees symbolic divisions (the tree of peaceful deities, then the tree of angry deities). "What he has thought and what he has done become objective: thought-forms, having been consciously visualized and allowed to take root and grow and blossom and produce, now pass in a solemn and mighty panorama, as the consciousness-content of his personality."‡ If the person is unable to recognize them, they disappear over the course of about three days, and through the same process of a supranormal birth in a subtle body, the dead person enters into the third bardo (Sidpa Bardo), which is the bardo of the search for rebirth. In this bardo, according to the possibilities of his meditation or of his projections, the alternative is presented of a supranormal rebirth through a transfer into a pure

---

*"This is evidenced, let us not forget, in the prescription to read and to re-read this book during one's life." From Evans-Wentz, *Tibetan Book of the Dead,* 151.

†Jung, "Commentaire psychologique," 171; *Gesammelte Werke,* vol. 11, § 842.

‡Evans-Wentz, *Tibetan Book of the Dead,* 29.

kingdom or paradise of the Buddha, or alternatively, through the desire of finding once again a body of flesh and blood, the alternative is presented of the impure choice of a samsaric matrix.* One sees that the initiation follows a *"climax a majore ad minus."*† Progressively, the offered possibilities descend from the Primordial Clear Light down to the Sidpa Bardo. All the way to the end the possibility is maintained to choose the Clear Light that appears, up to the definitive letting go, which fixes the incarnation in a human seed. From then on, it is what corresponds for us to the prenatal stage.

Already one glimpses the consequences of the overturning or backward motion that Jung is proposing with a view to making the *Bardo Thödol* an initiation for the Living Person. It would be necessary to move back up from the state in which the dead person was seen to be incapable of welcoming the teaching and of understanding the confrontation of the Chikhai Bardo and of the Chonyid Bardo, accentuating his irremediable descent and beginning to succumb to sexual Imaginings. He is attracted to dwellings where couples cohabit, until he falls prisoner to a uterus and is reborn in the earthly world. From the biological sphere, holding captive projections and Imaginings, he needs then to go back up "initiation-wise" until he reaches the state of perfect Awakening of which the Chikhai Bardo proposes the possibility (confrontation with the Primordial Clear Light).

Now it has already been shown that in our world of Western culture, the only initiatory process still being practiced is rational maieutics, which penetrates to the very depths of Consciousness, to the analysis of the Unconscious, of which Freud was the initiator.

With a powerful stroke of humor, the Jungian exegesis of the *Bardo Thödol* is going to reveal to us, by taking the level where

---

*Evans-Wentz, *Tibetan Book of the Dead,* 188.
†Jung, "Commentaire psychologique," 171; *Gesammelte Werke,* vol. 11, § 842.

Freudian analysis is located, the implied consequences for all those (of whom there is no shortage) who invoke the name of Freudian psychoanalysis, or just psychoanalysis.* The specific field of Freudian psychoanalysis is that of sexual Imaginings, of incompatible desires, of repression causing states of anxiety, and so on—in short, everything corresponding to the final chapter of the Sidpa Bardo. For the dead person, to whom the *Thödol* is addressed, it is a movement toward a uterine existence, which will be for him the point of departure of a new human existence that would be able to bring him closer to the state of awakening (*bodhi*). In contrast, for the Freudian analysand, under analysis he regresses, uncovering his unconscious content through infantile Imaginings *usque ad uterum*. Freudian analysis regresses even back to the memory of the intrauterine origin. But the analysis stops there, and it is a great pity it does, for one has the impression that with a little audacity, by going beyond the Sidpa Bardo, it could have stepped back into the Chonyid Bardo that preceded it. However, it cannot—first of all because the framework to which the biological and natural sciences are limited is not adequate, and because, in fact, it would have been necessary to admit what might be called a pre-existential existence (since prenatal is already applied to the intrauterine stage). Of course, Buddhism recognizes and professes this preexistence, but it is difficult for us to experimentally discover traces of experience of a subject in his preexistence given the present human condition.

This is why, while being the first Western attempt at exploring (from underneath) the area of the psyche corresponding to the Sidpa Bardo, Freudian psychoanalysis has remained there, enclosed in a Sidpa Bardo that it could not go beyond, since the Chonyid Bardo was barred to it.

---

*Jung, "Commentaire psychologique," 172–73; *Gesammelte Werke,* vol. 11, §§ 842–43.

This amounts to saying that whoever penetrates into the Unconscious
with exclusively biological presuppositions remains stuck in a sphere of
instincts without being able to go beyond it, similar to the dead person whose spiritual training is inadequate or null and who is therefore
condemned to always fall back and be locked into physical existence.
This is why Freudian premises could only lead to a purely negative valorization of the Unconscious ("this is nothing but . . .").* And, in summary, this state of affairs only reflects the modern conception of the
soul. This conception denounces the very level that it occupies when
it formulates against Jung's research the accusation of "psychologism."
Correlated with that we can be aware of the rationalist thinking that
caused Freudian psychoanalysis to degenerate into a dogmatism just as
rigid as those that any theology has ever been accused of.

Having now recognized this, the reversed-order reading of the *Bardo
Thödol* will allow us at present to discover its full meaning, "so that
our reading of it is situated and conducted on this side of life." And
from that point on also, the psychological investigation will be able
to penetrate into the Chonyid Bardo, without violating the sphere of
"occultism" in doing so. This progression measures the extent to which
Jung's complex psychology is differentiated from Freud's psychoanalysis and goes beyond it. It is also by situating ourselves on the Buddhist-
Lamaist plane that the Jungian exegesis will show us the blossoming

---

*Freud's use of this term is addressed in Laurens van der Post's *Jung and the Story of
Our Time* (pages 141–42): "Here, and in far too many other instances, was unmistak-
able evidence of a spirit which Jung saw as only part of an infinitely greater whole, and
not an end in itself. Yet Freud, who was doing his utmost to explain everything in terms
of a science where method and theory were one, ignored all this in Jung for years. Jung,
equally, suppressed his reservations about Freud and his reductive attitude of 'nothing
but'—a term derived from William James's statement in *Pragmatism*: 'What is higher,
is explained by what is lower and treated for ever as a case of 'nothing but'—nothing
but something else of an inferior sort.'"—*Trans.*

of its most characteristic concept, that of archetypes. Archetypes make their appearance in a phase of evolution and initiation of the psyche corresponding to that of the Chonyid Bardo.

Let us not forget that we are reading the *Bardo Thödol* in reverse order here. If we refer to the actual order of the book, it is through the lower plane, or stage, that we penetrate into the Chonyid Bardo. It is the place of Apparitions*—the place of Apparitions conditioned by karma, which means psychic residues inherited from previous existences. Depending on whether the influence is good or bad, the karma allows—or on the contrary prevents—the Consciousness from recognizing itself in the faces or figures that confront it in the course of its existence in the bardo. An experimental and psychological phenomenology cannot make pronouncements either for or against a thesis such as that of reincarnation any more than it is incumbent on it to prove "the existence of God," presuming that our epistemological premises were to make the task possible. However, its actual task is to discover the experimentally lived meaning of the professed thesis. It is in this way that karma can be understood as a theory of psychic heredity in the broadest sense—that is, including the life phenomena that are expressed essentially in a mental mode, just as other hereditary tendencies are felt physiologically.

(Note: Remember that E.W., the editor of the Bardo Thödol, *already suggested this interpretation—p. 52, referring to Huxley's opinion, unfortunately tainted with a biology of naturalist character—and p. 163, no. 2. Really*

---

*I am intentionally avoiding the use of the word *illusion*. Whatever one does, the concept remains a function of our theories of Knowledge. It is not the Apparition as such that is illusory; it is the meaning—the separated objectivity—that is conferred upon it by a consciousness that is powerless to recognize itself in the Apparition. It is to the extent that this Oneself is recognized that there is transcendentally *apparentia realis*. In the psychological realism of our day, the extent of recognition leads then to the deprecatory term *illusion*.

interesting note . . . However, he uses the word subconscious *for "true I." We have pointed out above the limited meaning of this word propagated by the popularization of "official" psychoanalysis, and this allows us to measure the extent to which our understanding can grasp Buddhist themes and the Jungian concept of the unconscious—that is to say, a transconsciousness. Not only the "I" as über Ich, for which narcissism could qualify. And the confusion would be disastrous if the Self were to represent the totality. Above, we have spoken about the way in which the "I" is only an experience in the present moment—in the sense that it is Non-I. In spite of page 27—no inheritance of prenatal, pre-existential individual memories, I think that the idea of successive existences preceding the present one doesn't let us ask a question that would be guided by a presentiment we can neither dismiss nor belittle. I am speaking about successive existences in many senses—higher condition, fall from Grace, or even an existence that is already human. Such an idea might be something like the persistence of an individual archetype that is perhaps not foreseen in the Jungian theory of archetypes, but which, discovered in the Zen/Honolulu/Suzuki, would have the sense that "one always inherits from oneself." What remains, indeed, is for the "I" to be connected again to the collective Unconscious in its definite relationship. In other words, "knowing" why a specific constellation of archetypes appears in a specific given individuality, in a "knowing," in a unique and typical assemblage (typical = individual = for each one his own archetype). In short, to determine what opens the way to individuation, and leads it to a conclusion, different each time in its individual spontaneity, as has been pointed out in the case of Zen. It seems to me that the individual archetype is linked to the idea of the spontaneous production of symbols. The idea of an individual archetype would correspond to the internal law regulating the structure and the development of the psyche as a whole, and, in an analogous way, to the monadism of Leibniz: affinity between Jung and Leibniz: I cannot insist here on this remark.)*

Jung now distinguishes a class of psychic inheritances that are not limited or conditioned either by family or by race. These inheritances are general arrangements within the mind, or more exactly Forms according to which the mind gives order to its contents and which we can designate as categories analogous to the logical categories of understanding, but with the difference that they are categories of the imagination. These Forms, having in themselves the character of typical Images, are technically designated by Jung as archetypes. Jung borrowed this term directly from the *Corpus Hermeticum*. These Forms, which are archetypes of the Imagination, reproduce spontaneously, without there being any need of a direct "tradition," as is evidenced by the multitude of cases where a positive historical line of descent would be unthinkable.

*(Note: A single example given by Jung [*Swedenborg and the *Bardo Thödol*]: "that the dead persons at first do not know they are dead." Mention here the curious reference from Swedenborg to the characters, conversations preserved in Tartary.)*

Thus, the Forms announce and denounce a universally present psychic structure that is differentiated and "inherited" within specific Forms. Every field of exploration offered to the religious sciences harbors inexhaustible treasures. These archetypes are like psychic organs (those of the prerational psyche, or, what might yet be better termed, the suprarational psyche). On all imagination, projection, and experience undergone, they imprint a determined direction and form in the same way as it is with the organs of the body. In their own sphere, the bodily organs are in no way simply data indifferent in potential but are rather "functional and dynamic complexes." In this way, we can economize the hypotheses and constructions that "historical explanation" has recourse to. Such an explanation is always moving on the surface, presuming unlikely transmissions and migrations (for example, the famous migration of symbols), looking for centers of dispersion here and there, and believing that all has been explained when, from cause to cause, from reduction to reduction, it believes it has rendered plausible a reduction from the same thing to the same thing.

The archetypes are the "dominant characteristics of the unconscious." The layer of the unconscious soul made up of these dynamic Forms is what Jung calls the collective unconscious, to which our two earlier Buddhist meditations have already led us. In Jung's books we are quite entitled to deepen his very fertile notion of archetypes, a notion that is structurally linked to his doctrine of the Unconscious and is related to the "I" and the Self. As for the moment in which it blossoms in the exegesis of one of the most extraordinary esoteric rituals of Mahāyāna Buddhism, there is good reason to stress this point further because of the extent to which it allows a truly captivating amplification of the karmic visions of the Chonyid Bardo, which henceforth can be read as a progressive initiation into the state of Awakening and addressed to living persons.

(Note: Once again do remember: opposite to Freudian regression toward the infantile state, this "regression" progresses toward the supreme moment of death, toward which the living person is moving, and from which the dead person progresses toward another existence. Keep in mind the two curves.)

Following this order of regression, the episodes of the *Bardo* begin by unveiling archetypes, karmic Images, first of all in their terrifying forms. The Chonyid state corresponds, in this sense, to an intentionally provoked psychosis. This involves dangerous things, infernal torture, and the threat of disintegration of this bardo body that composes or constitutes the subtle body that takes on the visibility of the soul in this intermediary existence. (The psychological equivalent would be schizophrenia in its destructive form.) Passing from the state of Sidpa Bardo to the state of Chonyid Bardo thus marks a perilous overturning of the efforts and intuitions of the conscious state, a sacrifice of the comfortable security in the obviousnesses of conscious egocentricity, leading to turning oneself over to the extreme insecurity of the apparently chaotic play of fantastic beings. However, this perilous traverse is not spared any "becoming oneself," since the transconscious whole of the Self includes the fearful lower and subterranean world, from which very often the conscious "I" has been freed only partially—just as it includes as well the higher, celestial world. This liberation of the subject in fact continues to be precarious insofar as it remains at the phase in which an object is posited (the "world in general"), on which the whole of the "bad" or the "good" is projected—it is an object in which one can vanquish this "bad" or change this "good." It is so handy to have this right here at hand since it guarantees the heavenly innocence of the subject! However, there have always been people—those "gnostics" whom we spoke about earlier—who have not been able to prevent themselves from understanding that the world and the living experience of this world have the nature of a symbol, of an image of something that lies deeply hidden in the Subject himself, in his own transsubjective reality. This is the deep presentiment that is being expressed in the Lamaist doctrine of the Chonyid, when it terms the experience of reality as "bardo." It is precisely in this state that the experience is the experience of the reality of thoughts—forms of thought appear as realities, faces, people . . .

In the order of backward progression that our reading is following, the frightful vision of the wrathful deities fades away and gives way to the vision of peaceful and friendly deities, each one in its respective group forming a mandala linked to a different center in the person, a Chakra.* We will take up the sequence here. However, we can only refer the reader to the extensive notes, commentary, and addenda of Evans-Wentz for the connection between the mystical psychology of Tantra and the grouping of divinities in the mandala (compare the

---

*We are not going to go into the sequence here, but we can refer the reader to the extensive notes and commentaries of Evans-Wentz on the links between the mystical psychology of Tantra and the grouping of divinities in the mandala. See Evans-Wentz, *The Tibetan Book of the Dead*, 217 et seq.

second addendum, p. 185 et seq.). Precisely to the extent in which yoga is to be understood as a "juncture" or "coupling" of a lower human nature with a divine higher nature whose responsibility is to direct the lower nature—a support on which the control of the mental process leading to the "achievement of Reality" depends—and precisely to the extent in which yoga can be considered to be a system of applied psychology, more than one book would be needed to delineate the correspondences with Jungian psychotherapy. Regarding these karmic visions, we would like especially to highlight the character of personal images. Visionary reality is most often treated lightly as consisting of personifications, as if the *fieri* was free of any problem. Further to this point, the final essay will in fact outline for us the most precious substantive added value for which one could hope. We have just seen that it is in the doctrine of archetypes that this added value shines.

However, there is one point that I want to emphasize. It is the extraordinary parallelism between what the Buddhist eschatology demonstrates (which is only a relative *eschaton*) in the *Bardo Thödol* and the doctrines and spiritual experiences attested by Swedenborg, especially in his book *De Caelo et Ejus Mirabilibus et Inferno*. We will put forward here the term *apparentiae reales* so as to avoid the ambiguous and inadequate term *illusion,* the use of which would bring to light an inadequate analysis of what *phainomenon* is. This is one of the technical terms of Swedenborg's lexicon used to characterize the Forms that appear externally as correspondences of a "lower" that, precisely, manifests necessarily in these Forms. These Apparitions are incommensurably more real than what we call the phenomena of our sensory world. This parallelism is not something I can dwell on here—a whole other book would be needed. The more or less convincing comparisons between Buddhism and Christianity have barely touched the surface of this "real" parallelism of which I am speaking. It seems significant to us in this regard that such an eminent master of Buddhism as D. T. Suzuki appreciated Swedenborg to the point of translating his work into Japanese and commenting on it. Did not our Balzac call Swedenborg "the Buddha of the North"? Already here, we would have an indication that the discovery of the "Giver of data" does not justify the alarm that the sensing of him causes in the natural consciousness. The naive, philosophical realism of this consciousness estimates that, in this case, God and the whole of metaphysical truth have been torn away from it. However, it is certainly acceptable that, for any realism instituting duality of thought and of being, and undergoing the dilemmas that the principle of noncontradiction opposes to it, an insoluble enigma is posed by Buddhist piety, which, at all degrees, is addressed to the multitude of Buddhas and Bodhisattvas. It is their compassion that has made this piety descend from their holy paradises. The pious cannot but see a contradiction in this. However, the Buddhist path moves between negation and the negation of negation; it moves in the Void, which is the pure transparency of the lapis-lazuli ground produced by Pure Land meditation.

From vision to vision, coming back now to each of the five Dhyani Buddhas, or meditation Buddhas—Buddhas of ecstasy with the deities composing their mandala, here we have the manifestation of the divine blue light of the central Dhyani Buddha:

(E.W. p. 98, quote the last § p. 90 in note and the end of the prayer on p. 91.)

"The Wisdom of the *Dharma-Dhātu,* blue in color, shining, transparent, glorious, dazzling, from the heart of Vairochana, as Father-Mother, will shoot forth and strike against thee with a light so radiant that thou wilt scarcely be able to look at it."* And perhaps then this passage from the initial phase of the Chonyid Bardo will ring like a

---

*Evans-Wentz, *Tibetan Book of the Dead,* 106.

reminder: "O nobly-born, when thy body and mind were separating, thou must have experienced a glimpse of the Pure Truth, subtle, sparkling, bright, dazzling, glorious, and radiantly awesome, in appearance like a mirage moving across a landscape in spring-time in one continuous stream of vibrations."*Perhaps that will no longer be the reminder of an initial instant *post mortem* of which the liberating invitation might not have been grasped, but rather it may be the presentiment of a supreme moment in which the initiatory death undoes the connection of death itself, and in which it is recognized that "thine own consciousness, shining, void, and inseparable from the Great Body of Radiance, hath no birth, nor death, and is the Immutable Light— Buddha Amitābha."† With this final vision, Karma is resolved, and with the Karma its illusions are resolved, and with the illusions all the inheritances and all the weight is resolved. Consciousness is liberated from the attachments that keep it the prisoner of objects, returning it to the initial atemporal state of dharmakāya—Body of Essence, essential Body.

From the Lamaist point of view, it is possible that the reversal operated by the reading of the *Bardo Thödol* in order to demonstrate a parallel to the sole initiation process still practiced in the West might be a secondary proposition. Also, the advice given to read and reread this book in the course of one's life must not be forgotten. And for our psychologist, the suggestion wasn't secondary to the extent that the book reveals an exceptional richness of archetypal content of the Unconscious. That something is "given," subjectively or objectively, so be it—and the *Bardo Thödol* gives nothing more than that. And one has a whole life to recognize who is the Giver of the pure data of Consciousness. Along with Jung, we must recognize that the old Lamaist sages may well have thrown a glance in

*Evans-Wentz, *Tibetan Book of the Dead,* 104.
†Evans-Wentz, *Tibetan Book of the Dead,* 96.

the direction of the fourth dimension and lifted off a veil from the grand secrets of life.*

Jung's commentary ends with a few lines of allusive density—as if his contemplation had come to a halt and he was looking for a direction between the lines. Upon being reminded of a negative appreciation and reaching out to be relieved of an unbearable weight, the following rejoinder gets formulated: the world of the Gods and holy spirits is "nothing other than the collective Unconscious in me." The statement that the Unconscious is the world of Gods and Spirits outside of me requires not just a few intellectual gymnastics but a whole human life—perhaps even many human lives of increasing fullness and completeness (Voll Stämmigkeit). Intentionally I am not saying *perfection*—because the "perfects" make quite other "discoveries."†Between these lines, a serious, decisive question is inserted. It includes a supreme response that can be sketched only at the end of a whole life. Perhaps C. G. Jung has proposed this response in his introduction to the *Tibetan Book of the Dead,* and perhaps the conclusion of *The Secret of the Golden Flower* will have us discover the secret connection in the encounters with Buddhist thought that we have made our way through here.

Das Tibetanisch Totenbuch aus der Englischen Fassung des Lama Kazi Dawa Samdup Herausgegeben von W. Y. Evans-Wentz, mit einem Psychologischen Kommentar von C. G. Jung (Zürich: Rascher Verlag, 1942), 32; Jung, "Commentaire psychologique," 180; *Gesammelte Werke,* vol. 11, § 855.

†*Das Tibetanisch Totenbuch aus der Englischen,* 35; Jung, "Commentaire psychologique," 181–82; *Gesammelte Werke,* vol. 11, § 857.

4

TAOIST ALCHEMY
On *The Secret of the Golden Flower**

The essay that we are beginning to examine here resulted from the friendly collaboration between C. G. Jung and the sinologist Richard Wilhelm, who sadly has passed away. The Chinese text translated by R. Wilhelm is the best study available of the religion of the Golden Elixir (Jindan zhi dao) whose founder from the eighth century of our era was the Taoist adept Lü Dongbin. The text attributed to him forms the basis of the book, and it is accompanied by later commentary. This material turns out to be heavily influenced by Mahāyāna Buddhism. And what's more: combining the two characters for "Golden Flower" into a single character results in the ideographic character for "light" (*guang*).† Other connections are glimpsed: in the first place, with the Persian religion of Light (there would have been Mazdean temples in several places in China) and, consequently, with all that proceeds from a mysticism that is actually

---

*Pinyin: *Tàiyǐ Jīnhuá Zōngzhǐ;* Wade-Giles: *T'ai I Chin Hua Tsung Chih.*
†C. G. Jung and Richard Wilhelm, *The Secret of the Golden Flower: A Chinese Book of Life,* trans. by C. F. Baynes (London: Kegan Paul, 1931), 9.

Iranian. And this is just as much the case also with Manichaeism, and with Nestorian Christianity. Certain resemblances in the ritual and liturgy have even impelled some researchers to identify the founder with the chronicler of the famous Nestorian Stele from Xi'an and to consider the religion of the Golden Elixir as a survival from the ancient Nestorians! Having this formidable complex before us, we must resist the temptation to pull in just any connection with these various religions of light. All we can do is to refer readers to Jung's introduction and Richard Wilhelm's translation. In addition, we might ponder the reasons for the lexicon chosen by Wilhelm, for example: "meaning" (German *Sinn*) being used for the word *Tao,* which is most often translated as "Way"; or equating *animus* with *hun* (*houen*) and *anima* with *po* (*p'o*), which are used in a sense that is very different from that in Jung's lexicon. Our very limited task here is, as before, to sketch the general outline of Jung's European commentary written for the translation done by his friend, and at the same time to accompany, in this meeting with typical oriental texts, the unfolding and inclusion of typical concepts from Jung's psychology. At this juncture, because of the Taoist origins of the text, it will not be surprising that it leads toward a result that supports and confirms Jung's extensive research on alchemy. The alchemical connection is present right from the initial data up to the final achievement, which is the Diamond Body.

The premises are relatively simple. Although there is no European language that provides a direct equivalent to the concept of the Tao, the representation being used in its treatment here restores its essential psychological content, which is to proceed consciously on a conscious path in which a double aspect is unified: Life and Essence, Essence and Life. *Essence* and *Consciousness* are interchangeable terms, just as in Mahāyāna Buddhism Light is the equivalent symbol to Consciousness. This is why the nature of Consciousness is always

expressed by means of analogies to Light. But that's just a term for
the couple Essence and Life. The state that maintains Consciousness
or Essence separated from Life corresponds to what Jung describes
as deflection or uprooting of Consciousness. A process of conversion signifies *ab initio* (Urerfahrung) a reunion with the intimate
laws of Life represented by the Unconscious, an achievement of
conscious Life. That is the Tao—the union of Consciousness and
Life. Already the alchemical process is entering in. To support this
reunion, a certain heat must be produced—that is, a raising of the
level of Consciousness, so that the abode of spirit/mind might be
illuminated.

This conjunction of opposites (Consciousness and Life, masculine
and feminine), operating on an upper plane of Consciousness is
neither something rational nor simply a matter of will. It is a process of psychological development that is never expressed and will
never be expressed except in symbols, among which the Diamond
Body is the symbol of the accomplishment of the Great Work. The
development of the individual personality cannot in fact be made
visible except in symbolic images, in spontaneous Imaginings that
form around abstract structures in which Jung willingly recognizes
real gnostic *arkhai*. These Imaginings can be expressed in thought,
formulating intuitively laws or principles dimly sensed. This is how
psycho-cosmic drama is born (theogonies and cosmogonies). They
can approach an iconography that is expressed in symbolic designs,
tending most often to reproduce a mandala-type Image. In the
East, the most beautiful of them are no doubt those of Tibetan
Buddhism, but Christian iconography offers numerous examples as
well. Most often, the design assumes the shape of a flower, or a cross,
or a wheel. In our case, to be exact, it is the Golden Flower, whose
secret our text promises to reveal, because it is in this flower that the

Diamond Body must develop. The flower is the Light of Heaven and the Tao.

While at the same time it is a mandala symbol, the design does not suggest only the mystical Flower but also its origin. It is the "bubble," the "germinal vesicle," the "dragon's castle at the bottom of the sea," the "heavenly heart," the "terrace of life," the "purple hall in the city of jade," and so on. The fascinating sequence of images seems inexhaustible. It is the *initium,* the "germinal vesicle," where Essence and Life, Life and Essence are again mixed together. The origin that appears thus as the present aim rests "at the bottom of the sea" in the darkness of the Unconscious. The analogy between the alchemist's furnace and the "germinal vesicle" is how "all the masters began their work." This is where "the lead of the water region" undergoes a refinement or sublimation process into noble Gold. And similarly, this is where we see the generation and growth of light up to the conjunction of Life and Consciousness—at first mixed together, then separated, then reunited! To the extent that the mandala reveals not only a form but also an origin and an aim, it is no longer a simple means of expression; it becomes an effective tool. It delineates a *templum,* a *temenos,* or an enclosure that protects the most intimate parts of the personality. The "magic" practices are only projections of psychic events, and that is why they produce effects and psychic reactions. Interest and attention are concentrated on this intimate and sacred domain, which is the source and aim of the soul. This intimate domain is precisely the center that achieves the unity of Consciousness and of Life (intensity and extensity). We must find it once again.

Because of this center, fixed in this way as a "creative point," there is an improved expansion of what our text describes as a circulation or a circuit of Light—that is, not simply a movement in a circle but something like a circumambulation that traces out the limits or the boundaries of a sacred space, thus making possible fixation and concentration. The "solar wheel is activated" means that everything that is peripheral is submitted to being directed by the center. This is why in this case movement is just another word for *master*. It is to tour oneself, to delimit oneself so that, under the direction of the center, entry is gained into all aspects of the personality. This amounts to designating self-knowledge as self-incubation. And in the end the sequence of images takes us to this archetype of the complete man that Plato drew as a perfectly spherical being—that is, total and complete, reuniting in himself both masculine and feminine (the essential elemental body awaiting resurrection in the land of Hurqalya).

(Recall the efforts to understand in a "realist" sense what a symbol of the Whole is, and not a simple iconographic need as a challenge to the anatomical cosmos of Greek beauty.)

What appears essentially as an experience and vision of Light that is shared by so many mystics, in this case furnishes Jung with an opportunity to bring in the most striking cases of the staying power of archetypes. We have here an experience familiar to some people, which Jung witnesses directly, and which seems to be an intense and "detached" state of Consciousness conforming to the reports of Saint Hildegard when she speaks of a state producing in the Light of Consciousness "regions of psychic events that are usually cloaked in darkness." This state of Consciousness that is "detached" or liberated from the object is exactly, in Buddhism, the fundamental Knowledge that, having ceased to objectify itself in fictitious realities, is itself its own object. It knows that its object does not differ from itself. And as such it proclaims the birth of the *pneumatikos* man, or the Diamond Body. Of course, the achievement of a unity such as this is beyond the power of conscious will, and this is why the process of individuation can never be attained other than with a symbol.

(Note: Remember what I have already said: "Individuation" coincides with the non-egoified Consciousness. Consequently, individuation could only be in apparent opposition to Buddhist terminology. It even highlights a neglected aspect of it. It is true that here too even there are also matters to be revised—a lexicon that has been too quickly accepted generally.

The union of the Fundamental Clear Light with the Clear Light produced as a "mixture of the Clear Light of the Mother and of the Child" has been shown earlier to be a unifying symbol in the doctrine of the Clear Light of Tibetan yoga. [Y.T. p. 237 already quoted on page 51.] Even as we are ending here, we will see that this symbol contributes to the final response sought by the question found in the last lines of the previously studied essay.)

To determine the path leading to this final response, it seems that a preliminary question might orient us. If we pose it, it is that we are already foreseeing the outcome that it will lead us to, and on which no doubt our paraphrase of Jung and Buddhism will depend. This question is formulated by a simple coming together of terms. That is, the terms "Conscious Life" or "Consciousness lived" being a designation of the state that is no longer separated from the object, since it has been integrated into itself. Do we need to ask then, "*Who is living this lived Consciousness?*" Certainly, all we are doing here is stating in an interrogative form certain final propositions in the commentary on the Golden Flower. Anticipating it then is to beat a path toward the conclusion where the fruit that is called forth when the Golden Flower opens must be named by the circuit, the circular movement of Light.

This Path is strewn with dangers and with indicators of salvation. To understand where they are located, do not forget that the psychic phenomenology has not decided upon the metaphysical truth or falsity of the content that it is analyzing. There is only one question being posed here to the phenomenologist. What is happening in the psyche? What psychic event forms an aspect and takes shape in its content? Of course, the search and response are already conditioned by the appreciation or lack of appreciation for the degree of being of the psyche itself. We have already alluded to that more than once here. In any case, it is at the level of being that is taken for granted here by the psyche that technical designations such as "autonomous psychic complex" and "fragmentary psychic system" must be understood. The contents of the psyche that are experienced and that are designated by these terms harbor presuppositions that necessitate the question posed above. The dangers themselves, which the contents of the psyche are readying, concern in a direct and decisive manner the fate and meaning of religious consciousness in general.

First of all, these dangers are those that the whole of the Buddhist teaching—especially the Mahāyāna and up to, *post mortem,* the *Bardo Thödol*—tries to guard against. It is the threat of disintegration that lies in wait for the individual consciousness, narrowly limited but intensely clear, when it meets the field of unlimited expansion of the collective unconscious. "Every fragment of thought takes shape and becomes visible in a color and form. All the powers of the soul reveal their traces." It is why the *Bardo Thödol* at each confrontation untiringly guards against this danger. The deities come from yourself. You must recognize all these Lights as the reflection of your own inner Light, and you must understand meeting them the way a son understands meeting his Mother.* It does not give way to any attraction toward the "dim Lights,"† nor does it prefer them to the dazzling Brightness. You must recognize yourself in the Brightness, not flee, and so on. Here too the eminent role of the mandala as an instrument of attainment in the psyche is understood. The mandala's delimiting concentrates and protects against dispersion and invasion. It is the confirming symbol of this individual totality, the concept of which will appear more and more indispensible to us. The Buddhist imagination might be able to conceive of innumerable multitudes of Buddhas and Bodhisattvas without there being an explosion or bursting in that Consciousness that in this way has been guarded and initiated to recognize itself. If the consciousness is not guarded by spiritual training, then crashes are produced that correspond to personality dissociation, all the interdependent mental turmoil of hallucinations, and so forth. Here too, it is a question of turmoil destructive to the personality's unity that the Freudian school tends to explain as being due to unconscious repression—always based on the dogma that the Unconscious is an effect or a derivative of Consciousness, whereas the order is the reverse. It is a grave error to presume that the psyche is identical to nothing more than the Consciousness and to confine it to that. It is a question here of content that develops spontaneously from the Unconscious and that the Consciousness is no longer able to assimilate. The theory of repression no longer has any meaning in such a context.

Conversely, if taken too far, might not the reduction of the danger of dissociation lead to another threat? We are speaking here of

---

*Evans-Wentz, *Tibetan Book of the Dead*. [Corbin references page 105, but that page number seems to come from an edition other than the English one. —*Trans.*]
†Evans-Wentz, *Tibetan Book of the Dead*, xlv.

extremely subtle emotional states that, because they are constituent elements of the mental personality, necessarily have the character of persons. The more complex they are, the more they have the character of a personality. If dissociative tendencies were inherent in the human psyche, "fragmentary systems" would never have become autonomous and there would never have been a world of Gods and Spirits. On the other hand, does that imply that balance is to be found in a process that leads the ancient Gods to the state of personified ideas and finally by reducing them to the state of abstract ideas? I really think that, here, Jung is bringing to the spiritual state of our times a diagnosis leading to fertile reflection. It is through ignorance of the Unconscious psyche and through the pursuit of an exclusive cult of Consciousness that our era has become so completely atheist and profane. The sacred and the sense of hierophanies do not arise from intentions of the rational Consciousness. In fact, the true religion of our times is a monotheism of the Consciousness, an exclusive possession of that Consciousness, accompanying a rejection that fanatically denies the existence of fragmentary autonomic systems. In that, certainly, we differ from the doctrine of Buddhist yoga. And we find a sign in the fact that we deny that such fragmentary systems can be experienced, and that, at the same time, we might justifiably judge Buddhism by imposing on it our categories of monotheism, polytheism, and pantheism. It might contain all that, but also none of all that.

Jungian psychology has taken on the task of restoring the essential reality of both this universe and the soul—a reality that absolutely belongs to them and that is irreducible to the categories of the world such as our rational Consciousness has constructed it. However, swept along in their ignorance of the universe and the soul, our human sciences believed themselves capable of intellectually understanding and criticizing religious realities. *(Bring in here perhaps a note on synchronicity and astrology.)* It would seem that if our human-kind believed in demons, it was as in something external, which we might have finally experienced or proved their nonexistence. This was the naive recognition of the powerful internal effect of fragmentary autonomic systems that are always present, always working away, because the fundamental structure of the Unconscious does not change or vary with the fluctuation of the official Consciousness. "The names have been criticized but the effect continues—only it is no longer understood." Since it is no longer understood, it is projected. The disturbing effects are attributed to some bad intention or other that is external to ourselves, most likely the intention of our neighbor. From this there arise collective illusions, appetite for revolution, and warlike rattlings—in short, all the mass psychoses. If the madness consists in being possessed by an unassimilated unconscious content, what hope of assimilation would still remain when, precisely, our Consciousness denies the existence of such content? We have become perhaps too grown up for words with no content but not "for psychic realities that were responsible for the birth of the Gods." We are not any the less possessed by the content of our psyche than if this possession came from the Gods.

Here we now come to a fundamental religious reality couched in entirely new terms. Its correct hermeneutic is necessary to religious phenomenology and decides its fate, its success, or its failure. The principal question posed by fragmentary autonomous systems is that of the necessity and process of personification. *Personification* is a word that we abuse. We believe that we can dispense with an in-depth analysis of a divine figure. We say, "It's a personification of . . ." and we think that explains everything. The essence however remains in question: Where does the *fieri* that makes up the process of personification come in? These "personages" are not of our making or of our invention. Their valorization by Jung is of incalculable consequence. It is not we who have personified these powers of the psyche—that is, it is not we who construct our own personal figures. They have a personal nature *ab initio*. We have here an aspect of "classification by category" that corresponds to the character *a priori* that the archetypes have—a character of pure understanding. Once this is understood, we can grasp the full extent of the vanity to be found in the reproach sometimes addressed to Jungian psychology, the reproach that it is restoring a "mythology" or "hypostases." The "personifications" are not of his invention—they are inherent in the nature of phenomena. Note that if a given category is not an object of knowledge, even less is the nature of a "fragmentary system," in a transcendental sense, an object of Knowledge. What we understand and experience of this is the representation of our own personal nature.* And as we finish we will see that this will be of final, decisive importance as to the transcendental nature of the Self and what is in fact experienced.

The experimental significance of the "personifications" appears in the process of transmutation of reality that is presupposed by the state of "absolute" Consciousness, finally liberated from the object of its projections (integration). Paradoxically, we might say, I believe, that the more the object is detached—as autonomous in relation to Consciousness—the less the Consciousness can detach from it. Thus, there would be a first degree in which, since their reactivity to Consciousness is not recognized, and consequently is

---

*Compare with C. G. Jung and Richard Wilhelm, *The Secret of the Golden Flower: A Chinese Book of Life,* trans. by C. F. Baynes (London: Kegan Paul, 1931), 118–19.

entirely "projected," these "personifications" are proportionately more activating and subjugating and have the reality of an absolute object. Rationally criticizing them or denying them does nothing but sanction the nonrecognition and their domination. There is a degree in which they are recognized as real—in relation to the soul that is experiencing them. We might say, I believe, that an initial phase of interiorization leads them back to their origin. In religious terms, this corresponds to the formation of a faith. And after that, a degree of perfect interiorization comes in which I don't think it is necessary to term them unreal, because nonobjectivity does not mean nonreality. And if the Consciousness detaches itself from their formal content and is no longer possessed by them—because they are already experienced in their pure psychic reality—the ultimate question is intuited or glimpsed: Who is working away in the *fieri* that is producing the personages? Who is personifying the personifications? *Quid* of the spontaneity of this *fieri* [is present] so that the soul meets these figures as having been always there, *ab initio*—that is, well before the conscious psyche knew about them?

Once psychic reality has been understood for what it actually is, you know that in accepting it there is nothing to fear—but no, quite the contrary! You might fall back into some demonology or other, or into a primitive mythology. If one agrees that, with the threat of being led into a state of mental tension (a forerunner of psychosis) it is essential to recognize the figures that rise up from the unconscious—or break through from the horizon of the transconsciousness (the dignity of the factors having a clean and spontaneous efficiency)—then one will readily agree that, among these figures, the one who personifies the Unconscious or the transconsciousness in general is of primordial importance. This figure that is in the dominant role in the whole of his psychology is, as we know, the one that Jung designates alternatively as *anima* in a man or *animus* in a woman. Here too let us recall that *anima* represents personal nature. It personifies a system of the psyche that, in its transcendental sense, remains beyond the limits of experience and that we can only relate to its sources. What needs to be emphasized here is the extent to which this *imago animae*—insofar as its encounter is a decisive stage in the process of individuation—holds, all in all, the secret of the Golden Flower. This personification of the Unconscious is initiated just as much under the inner aspect of our dreams, fantasies, and visions as under the external aspect of the actual person on whom it is projected. These two aspects reflect back to the subject his own inner Image that he carries in himself of the opposite or complementary sex. The meeting with the *imago animae* is, for each human being, the moment in which he will become aware of the feminine or masculine part of his psyche that he carries within himself and which, in our Western civilization that is totally oriented toward the patriarchy, has been for each individual so deeply buried in the Unconscious. This is the moment of initiation to oneself in which the union and reciprocal action of the masculine and the feminine must attain, beyond the physical plane where the posterity of the flesh is perpetuated, those depths of soul in which each one of the couple is able to conceive, one with the other, that spiritual child who will ensure for his or her spiritual being a duration that the time of our world neither measures nor limits. This meeting presumes that the task of adaptation to external reality has ended for the Consciousness. Then there begins the most important stage, that of adapting to the inner— each one's confrontation with the part of his own psyche that is of the opposite sex. The activation of the archetype of the *imago animae* is therefore a supreme event. It is the undeniable sign that the second part of the life has begun. Now this spiritual child born of the conjunction with the *anima* whose secret stirs Consciousness is something we are going to see depicted in the archetype of the Diamond Body—the fruit that must spring forth from the Golden Flower. All that remains to be done is to beat a path toward this attainment. Two stages move alongside this development: the dissolution of the mystical participation that was oppressing a consciousness in the grip of unconscious projections and the formation of a new focus for the personality. Here too, indeed, our psychology and our spiritual therapy are able to reveal their effectiveness to ensure for the soul a treatment and a well-being similar to those that the ancient wisdom of the East was pursuing, and further, to bring a sudden increase in valorization of this wisdom through an exegesis of the soul, without falling into the trap of a literal reproduction.

What the adept of the "Golden Elixir" is initiated into is the concentration of Light on the most intimate region, and the liberation of himself from any attachment, which means bringing about a cessation of the intermingling of Consciousness with things and objects. In other words, what we're speaking about here is a penetration of the Unconscious, which in fact leads to a cessation of the domination, and also of the magic power that things claim to have. It is not that the fullness of the world has lost any of its richness or its beauty but rather that the Consciousness is empty and nonempty. Empty because the images of things have given up their tyranny; nonempty because they have not ceased to exist. They have been interiorized, but instead of being put up with, the Consciousness simply contains them all because it has transmuted them by recognizing in them its own Image. The consciousness has become pure vision, detached from objects. It is now the object of Consciousness that is no longer detached: Consciousness itself is contemplating its own Act (Consciousness becomes resolved in visions, the disc of the moon floats all alone). Let us measure the distance we have traveled along the Way in reference to this mystical participation that C. G. Jung is evoking here. Its technical designation remains attached to the name [Lucien] Lévy-Bruhl. To the extent that the nondifferentiation of object and subject depends on their difference not having risen into Consciousness, it is an Unconscious state of identity that prevails— and to the extent that the Unconscious is projected into the object, it is the object that is interjected into the subject. Civilized man is not that far removed from this primitive Unconscious. Does he not recklessly accuse others of things that he does not see are in himself? Is he not "magically" affected by innumerable people, things, events, and circumstances? But if the unconscious were recognized—that is to say, if it were able to be experienced in such a way that its exigencies were admitted side by side with the conscious exigencies—then "the whole center of the personality changes its position. It ceases to be in the ego, which is only the center of the Consciousness, and it situates itself in what we might call a virtual point between the Conscious and Unconscious. This new center can be designated as the Self."

Here it seems that we are coming to the climax. The whole Buddhist effort tends to abolish and surmount the egoified "I." The whole effort of in-depth psychology is to go beyond the limited ego at the center of the conscious psyche and to free from its casing the jewel that concentrates the lightning strikes that pierce the night of transconscience. One way or another the rupture of the darkness of the Unconscious or of the "unscience" turns upside down the perspective in which illusory and ready-made Knowledge holds sway. Consciousness, liberated from the world, also liberates a world without limits. This anaphora *ab imo* that rises toward itself is a preparation for death in the initiatory sense of the word. It means taking the spiritual existence as an aim. It means preparing the birth and survival of the psycho-spiritual body, the Diamond Body that is the fruit of the Golden Flower, in which alone there is glimpsed, in the end, the attainment of the personality as a whole. The transmutation that such a birth presumes and announces is something that the Westerner had some notion of in antiquity, notably in the initiations of the mystery religions. What was called the birth of spiritual man designated this same psycho-spiritual event.

Isn't all that in harmony with Christianity? Quite rightly, Jung is putting us on guard here against the total misunderstanding that would take Christian ascetic faith and morality along with our Buddhist texts to be similar treatments tending toward comparable ends. There is a very great distance between the sublimation with which the wisdom of the Great Vehicle intends to overcome the passions and the violent repression of the instincts that has plagued our spirituality in general and has consummated the divorce between soul and body (as a ransom perhaps for a reconciliation between soul and mind that have been emaciated in the intellect). This repression has led us today in return to be subjected to the terrible shock of resentment and transference that analytical psychology is called upon to resolve! We have just evoked the mystery religions, but we have done so to remind ourselves that today there are no longer either initiations or mysteries. We can be delighted that the mystery has been profaned; we can proclaim it from the rooftops. However, we see where it has left us. On the long path of history have we not misplaced more than one christianity? For the exegete of the soul, the conspicuousness that the official forms of the present time enjoy does nothing to confer upon them the privilege of an exclusive authenticity nor the justification of being at the culmination of a providential evolution.

We would need to deepen the motifs of the great fear and the viciousness of the official institution mobilized against gnosis and against everything that, in the course of the ages, recalls or revives gnosis. Doubtless, in so doing we would delineate the motivations for this pain and suffering that characterizes Western Christianity, mainly since the Middle Ages, and which was profoundly foreign to early Eastern Christianity. If it is true that a gulf yawns between the regions of the soul where we glimpse "the purple hall of the City of Jade," where the Golden Flower grows, and the regions where the Image of a suffering and humiliated Christ is fostered, the contrast is no less striking than that between the Image of the Cross and the secret of the Cross of Light to which a *Christos-angelos* initiates the disciple in the *Acta Johannis*. Here we have quoted an apocryphal book. However, "apocryphal" means not inauthentic but hidden, mysterious. These are the books that, significantly, the official institution repressed as a secret that was forbidden for anyone to read. Strange how that resembles the refusal to recognize other rights than those of the religions of the conscious psyche, the consequences of which Jung tirelessly reminds us! And these books reveal something in common among all forms of gnosis, which includes, as Welt religion, Valentinian and Manichaean gnosis, gnosis in Islam, and Buddhist gnosis—of the Great Vehicle and the Diamond Vehicle. One of their traits in common is to grasp facts and realities in the spontaneity of the consciousness that perceives them and conceives of them, and not in the materiality in which they are externalized— that is to say, to grasp them as visions. A Christian gnosis, for example, will grasp the life of Christ as and within the ensemble of visions that each of the disciples had of Christ; it will not be understood as a sequence of data that is external, material, and identical for all persons. Since the scene for these facts and realities is in the soul, and since the pure inner reality seems so evanescent and precarious for anyone not finding support in the external object, all that has been characterized as "docetism" (*dókēsis,* literally "apparition," "phantom"). Conversely, we are inclined to say that all these "docetists" were perhaps the first phenomenologists. It is not a question of a historical trial to be defended or accusations to be brought. It is still the case that the process of the de-christianization of the world poses crucial questions, the meaning of which naturally varies with each person to whom that process is addressed. However, as we consider all the christianities lost to the soul in the course of Christianity's history, we might wonder if, for modern man—in the case of the de-christianized man of our times, who is post-Christian and still religious—would a rediscovery of Christianity pose very different problems for him than would the encounter with any other religion, such as Buddhism, for example?

This rediscovery, in any case, would not result from either theological arguments or from a so-called adaptation that would simply bend religious things to a frenetic socialization, which our era inflicts on all things. It requires this exegesis of the soul according to which Jung's analytical psychology has been developed *(Reminder: I used this expression for the characteristic process of ta'wīl. Compare my Avicenna and the Visionary Recital),* since perhaps this exegesis might allow us to respond to the objections of the non-exegetes. Let it be understood: with Eastern Sages, their attitude* is as great and indubitable as it is disrespectful toward their metaphysics. This disrespect is precisely the frequent accusation of literalist exegetes when meeting those who are not satisfied with a spiritual exegesis

---

Secret of the Golden Flower, 129; *Gesammelte Werke,* vol. 13, § 74.

and whom they accuse of allegorizing. For the latter, without an exegesis of the soul, the exegesis of texts is meaningless. The texts that are relevant for psychology are all the dogmatic, metaphysical, mythological, and so on, statements. It is not for psychology to incorporate these textual data but to discover the source and motivation to which they respond and which they express. Otherwise, one might wrap oneself in mystery, profess with authority any esotericism that took one's fancy, but in so doing one would be left with an esotericism that is as official, a dogmatism as superficial as all those to which one makes this reproach. And God knows how certain esotericisms of this kind are all the rage in our times! Of these sublime and abstract statements we must ask, "Where is all that taking place?" If this question is responded to by qualifying it as psychological, it is a pitiful response. Could anyone be silly enough to think that each one of us could end up putting "our soul in our pocket"? When Meister Eckhart or Angelus Silesius profess the necessity of a never-ending divine birth in the soul, will they be accused of psychologizing? Ultimately, this reproach is only the corollary of an abstract metaphysical pretension that, while professing an absolute and inaccessible deity in the human experience, imagines that it is possible to talk about the deity just the same. Will it surprise us then to come up against agnosticism? Agnosticism at least recognizes quite well the danger of this exegesis of the soul, of this psycho-exegesis that leads the soul to itself when the agnosticism accuses the exegesis of restoring Neoplatonic hypostases, for example! But the substance of such hypostases would in any case be consubstantial with the soul. If someone finds some other hypostasis, may they please explain where, and from where, it is experimentally given. If the Jungian exegesis of the soul is submitted to the crossfire of dogmatic philosophers and agnostics then it is really a good sign.

His exegesis naturally is suffering the fate of something fundamentally new and promising. It is not two attitudes of the soul (believing and knowing) that it claims to reconcile, but the soul itself with its own faith and its own knowing. What comes out from that is not a unilateral knowing but rather a knowing that has been experienced and of which the function corresponds to the path of the individuation process of "he who knows." All of that has been accomplished following a path of scientific psychology. It is clear then that we have here a promise, an *aurora consurgens*.

And it is this aurora that illuminates our psychologist's meeting with the East, and specifies to this looking east what its task can be as an exegesis of the soul. No longer can it be a simple exegesis of texts to satisfy a purely historical knowledge that feels self-satisfied when it has "placed" the fragments of the soul on the surface of Time and adjusted them like the pieces of a puzzle. This aurora transfigures the East into a symbol of the soul in search of itself. Increasing our familiarity with the spiritual East and Eastern spirituality must be for us the symbolic expression par excellence of the inner event that puts us in contact with strange and foreign elements in ourselves.*

(Note: Recall this meaning of the Orient in Avicenna and Suhrawardi).

To want to reject the premises of our own culture, assimilating the East through a purely literal exegesis, would be the surest means of provoking a new uprooting of consciousness. It is starting from our own soil that we have to set out toward this East, and it is along the way of this pilgrimage that we will discover answers to the questions: Who is the one living through the experience of consciousness? Who is the Giver of the data? And, consequently also, the response to the question that hangs mysteriously in the allusion

---

*Secret of the Golden Flower, 128; Gesammelte Werke, vol. 13, § 72.

with which the psychological commentary on the *Bardo Thödol* concluded. The discovery can always be picked up again in new statements. I believe that they all converge toward the realization that the psyche is a world in which the conscious "I," the *ego,* is contained.* And when this secret connection between the psyche and this "I" moves up into Consciousness, it finds its expression beside so many other related symbols of our own Latin alchemists, as well as in the Diamond Body, the indestructible spiritual body that develops in the Golden Flower. Experienced as an objective psychic fact, this body is first of all projected and expressed in images borrowed from forms supplied by the experience of organic life: fruit, embryos, child, living body. Even more directly, the transmutation of the subject would appear in the startling substitution of an *ego vivor* for *ego vivo*—"I am lived." The truth of the ego attained in its *significatio passiva,* which is specifically its action, and which measures the whole distance with respect to the former egoifying "I": from this it becomes clear in what way the Buddhist negation of the ego is not the nihilism that our intellect sees as the only alternative. Let us understand clearly that this significatio passiva is not at all equivalent to affirming the condition of the creature, the created being. "Creationism" is only a philosophical mode of expression derived from a particular mode of experiencing this mode of being. The illusion as to the higher powers of the conscious mind is what has led to this opinion: it is I who is living (*ego vivo*). From the moment that the authority of the transconscious psyche is recognized, this pretension and this seclusion are broken. It is this transconscious psyche that is living me, the psyche of which my ego is a part, and this psyche is the totality that I can find once again, not by mixing with it but specifically by the process of individuation (the great misunderstanding of the word *collective*

---

*Secret of the Golden Flower, 131; Gesammelte Werke, vol. 13, § 76.

I must say I have now understood). This process is exactly the climax of activity of this living psyche. From that moment on there also appears a détente, a calming, a "relaxation" of all the impossible responsibilities—for the primitive beings that we are, yet civilized— that are dragged in by our mystical participation in various kinds of objects (ideological, social, political, maniacal, and so on). In Christian terms: "awareness of being a child of God freed from the voice of the blood."* In terms of our Chinese text: "whoever attains the pinnacle of achievement returns to the beauty of Nature."† Here we are able to understand what ordeal must be undergone to overturn the banal, tainted proposition of psychologizing according to which the world of the Gods is nothing more than the Unconscious in me: in "the unconscious is the world of the Gods outside of me" (at the end of the *Bardo Thödol*). But perfected beings, we have been told, make other discoveries. And perhaps we are very close to that. This total change in intimate feeling, this détente and calming promised by the revealed presence of the subject that is living me, can be compared to the change experienced by a man to whom a child is born,‡ with the essential difference involved in a spiritual birth, and with the difference that this child is specifically me. Certainly we can evoke the famous words of Saint Paul—"It is Christ who lives in me"—were it not for the danger of identifying with the form of the Pauline experience (and its repetitions in Christianity), this fundamental experience of which the symbols show the diversification. "It is as if a higher spiritual being in human form was invisibly born in the individual in the manner of a spiritual body destined to serve as his abode."§ It is the same psychic event that is expressed in the Image, "re-clothed

---

*Compare with *Secret of the Golden Flower*, 133; *Gesammelte Werke*, vol. 13, § 77.
†Compare with *Secret of the Golden Flower*, 131 and 133; *Gesammelte Werke*, vol. 13, § 78.
‡Compare with *Secret of the Golden Flower*, 132; *Gesammelte Werke*, vol. 13, § 78.
§ Compare with *Secret of the Golden Flower*, 132; *Gesammelte Werke*, vol. 13, § 78.

in new clothing" (for example, in the Acts of Thomas), because it is impossible to express this renewal in rational concepts. Without being "deposed," the individual experiences the feeling of being "replaced," being taken in charge by some secret and loving higher (some invisible center), thanks to which his life is henceforth lived in the calm and devotion of this free dependency described by Schleiermacher. "Free in the most loving separation," according to what Nietzsche has written.

(It would be necessary here to cite Hermas, the angel to whom he has been confided. That is the space of the angel. What baptism signified. And with the gnostics.)

This transformation of the "I" that appears in the experience of its *significatio passiva* places us on the way to an adequate representation of the state of Buddhist Awakening. *(See the very beautiful pages by Suzuki in Essai IV, p. 88 et seq.—psychology of passivity—"The suppression of the "I" does not mean its complete annihilation, but rather its perfect disposition to welcome a higher power." p. 89, and notably in the chapter, "La passivité dans le bouddhisme de la Terre pure" [Passivity in Pure Land Buddhism] p. 101 et seq.)* And it is striking that this recognition is experienced as a birth—or rebirth—appearing always in the symbol of the formation of a perfect body or *corpus spirituale. (Quote here Lanka p. 71 and 61–62, in fol. ZB.)* More specifically still, the idea of this birth and of its symbols has as its frame of development a sophiology of which the archetype has been vivified and activated in very diverse religious spheres. The substitution of an *ego vivor* for the *ego vivo* irresistibly evokes a comparison with the essential development of Baader's thought: "Because God, in thinking me, penetrates my thought and I find myself thought by Him—*cogito, qui cogitor*—the thought of God is impenetrable to my thought, whereas a being placed below me is penetrated by me thinking of him, without my being penetrated by him." *(Cited in Susini III, 192–93.)* At this point he has just substituted a *Cogitor ergo sum* for the Cartesian *Cogito ergo sum*. I believe that Baader's effort, even though pursued on the specific plane of his personal theosophy, is in resonance with Jungian analysis, which, of course, as a general exegesis of the soul, cannot be linked to the context of Baader's premises. But there is more.

5

CONCLUSION
The Self and Sophia

Structurally, Baader's *Cogitor* seems linked to a representation that is no less dear and essential to him among all his others: that of Sophia. Through his Fall, man left Sophia together with whom he ought to have dwelled—the "woman of his youth" as Solomon said— and Sophia left man. She returned to the uncreated state, and man was left pinned down in his purely creatural state. And yet, this "celestial humanity," in the far distance where she resides—unreachable— remains a beacon in the night of fallen humanity. She is his angel and his guide. She is the *nisus formativus:* the supreme instinct and the supreme ideal of the entry into forms. Her image corresponds so well to the archetype of *anima-animus* that as a sidereal phantasmagoria, the Virgo Sophia, man's angel and guide, appears to the lover in the form of the beloved and appears to the beloved in the form of the lover. We have seen that taking the spiritual existence as an aim is to hold to the entry into forms and the higher-level existence of the spiritual body, the Diamond Body. In the same way also for Baader, the supreme aim of love, which goes beyond the sphere of time, is the organic rebuilding—the incarnation—for the two lovers, of the divine Image of God or of the Virgo Sophia, which has become for man the incorporeal spirit by means of which the two lovers engender once again children of God. Through the fault of man, Sophia has become an incorporeal spirit. The Virgo Sophia aspires and strives to regain possession of her "corporality," which is understood to be a "spiritual" corporality. The only one to achieve this aspiration is he in whom Christ has begun to take form. Thus Sophia is the Virgo Mother of the invisible mystic child.

And this ongoing incarnation, operating through the mystery of Sophia and granting the wish of all mystics *(Recall Silesius. "Of what use is Gabriel to me . . .")*, is the last word of the response. We know who the subject of life is—the Giver of the data. We have recognized the sense in which what is outside of me is lower than what is inside me. And we have also recognized the sense in which what is inside me is outside me—that within which I am contained, thought, and experienced. The *Commentary on the Secret of the Golden Flower* ends with a last caution, which in the end referred us again to this idea of the spiritual exegesis that we have enunciated above. Since it is an exegesis of the soul and not a literal exegesis of a text, it can only put us on guard against any imitation—a literal Imitation. From this there arises a comparison between the way in which the oriental sage treats the diamond as a central symbol *(perhaps a note G.F. 134—the idea of redemption depends on the works of each—and Swedenborg)* and the *Imitatio Christi* that the West has experienced and that is linked to a concrete humanity of the flesh and to the personality and historicity of Christ. And perhaps it happens that, fixated on the model incarnating the deepest meaning of life, we might forget to make real the deep meaning present in ourselves—and perhaps it is not so uncomfortable to renounce one's own real meaning? If Jesus had done as much, would Christianity ever have been? However, were a man to dare to proclaim and be what he really is were he to really understand the meaning of what he does, then he will be one of those who steps out of the rank and file, and he will be one who, without regard for the suffering, makes real the symbol of Christ.*

The European commentary on *The Secret of the Golden Flower,* which allows us to glimpse the practical consequences of any exegesis of the soul, appeared in its first edition in 1929. The psychological commentary on the *Bardo Thödol,* the ending of which left us with a foretaste of an expectation, appeared in 1935. Since then, the questions that flowed together in the final pages of one or the other essay did receive their ultimate answer while at the same time draining away all other questions that might have been left hanging in the totality of Jung's work. I think that the answer is specifically Jung's *Antwort auf Hiob (Answer to Job),* which offers the most personal, and nevertheless unconditionally courageous, answer—one which is a challenge for an epoch that is so afraid of the individual. For very few indeed are the men of science who engage their whole soul in their science and who are aware that their experience fatefully engages the souls of other individuals! The book was a sign of contradiction for some and an inexhaustible source of contemplation for others. We can do nothing else but refer the reader to this *Response to Job* at the conclusion of this paraphrase, which guides us in that direction. *(Reference Antwort and my article "Sophia.")* It is right here that we find ourselves present at the unfolding of a human drama that repeats in each individual. The process of that unfolding is revealed only to an attentive psychic phenomenology. How is it that in the deity's divesting himself of his shadow side, it is man himself

---

Secret of the Golden Flower, 134–35; *Gesammelte Werke,* vol. 13, § 78.

that the deity then unburdens of this shadow? Simultaneously, God is born to man and man is born to God as Filius Sapientiae, son of Sophia. This co-birth—an event of the soul and not of the external, material history—initializes the reign of Sophia and her mediating work as "defender and witness or advocate in Heaven." Do realize that our evoking Baader above was not a mistake. Christ's incarnation is the prototype that, progressively, the Holy Spirit transfers to the human creature. Man is born anew as Filius Sapientiae: he through whom the Holy Spirit accomplishes divine anthropomorphosis. It is understandable that the concept of this "ongoing incarnation" (the expectation and hope of so many mystics) sounds terrible to orthodox dogmatic individuals. It is probable that it is postulating a concept of incarnation that is different from the theology of the Councils, which also had their deep motivations, the analysis of which remains to be done. It is also probable that many individuals, discovering the concept of an incarnation in a spiritual body, accord themselves the facile triumph of reproaches addressed to the docetists (these first phenomenologists). Now, specifically in this latching-on of the consciousness to the material manifestation of the objective historical fact in the past (which it thematizes without realizing it), there is nothing but the symptom of this form of consciousness that has been illustrated all along. And to understand that it is a matter of an attitude that originates in unexplored psychic depths, one need only realize the pandemonium engendered by a book like *Answer to Job* or simply by an updating of the Christology of *Christos-angelos*. We are not suffering under any illusion that we are not yet near to understanding one another about this!

This essential aspect remains: What *Answer to Job* configured and materialized and what the Pure Land meditator characterized as the diaphanous ground of lapis lazuli, would it not be a Sophianic

Christianity that would remind us in the present and valorize the intentions and foreseeing of all Sophiologies? The word can be used in the plural. It is not from Christianity or from the souls of mystics that there springs forth a bearing witness to the eternal Sophia. There is a Mazdean Sophiology *(compare with Terre celeste, p. 31–81)*; there is a Manichean Sophiology; there is even one in Islamic gnosis. The exegesis of the soul can only call on all these witnesses. However, our paraphrase was developed on Buddhist themes. It is fitting that it finishes by mentioning the symbolism that associates Liberating Knowledge with representations of a Sophology that is specifically Buddhist. Earlier we have already spoken about the co-birth in each Bodhisattva of the state of awakening to things as vision and of a subtle body of thoughts—and of how Buddha nature is the true center in a way that is quite different from the *ego* of *Cogito*. The teaching of the *Tibetan Book of the Dead* brings in the psychic process, thanks to which there arises the dawn of Clear Light. This is the Clear Light mother of which the recognition—the result of deep meditation—is compared to meeting someone you have previously known. It is called the mixture of the Clear Light of the Mother and of the Child. *(Compare above and Y.T. 236–37.)* The symbols, which are never by chance, sketch out a figure whose features are clarified elsewhere—for example, there where the Bodhisattva is invited to undertake preparations and to embellish and adorn his body as an abode worthy of receiving *Prajñā,* the Wisdom-Sophia (as in the Song of Songs). And there is a whole Buddhist literature that tends to consider *Prajñā-Sophia* as the mother of Buddhas, in the sense that it is through her that all Buddhas come to their Buddha nature and obtain supreme and perfect enlightenment and that it is she who therefore engenders Buddhas. Buddhas subsist by merging with her, and numerous stupas are dedicated to her glorification. This tendency has its full flowering in the Shaktism of Adamantine

Buddhism (Vajrayāna, Diamond Vehicle), where each Buddha and Bodhisattva is conjoined with a feminine deity, which is his Shakti, his creative Energy.

(Lamotte, M., pps. I, 280 et seq. for example for Shakti, and Tantra somewhere in Eliade. Cf. already in B.T. the feminine Bodhisattavas in the mandalas.)

There is nothing surprising about the alternating of aspects (mother, lover) under which the relationship to the essential Feminine appears. It is a relationship that is so compelling that it overcomes the metaphysical obstacle by transmuting it. For example, in the case where the Vairochana Buddha is perceived as a "Universal Body of Essence-ness," it means that he cannot be "engendered" by anyone else. But then the "Mother of the Buddhas" will be called "Eye of the Buddha," because she is the Perfection of Wisdom who gives birth to Omniscience. And it is thus because this Eye of Omniscience allows the Buddhas to discern the various needs of beings to be saved, and to engender subsequently all the Mothers, the various forms, the hypostases or manifestations appropriate to the various categories of beings. *(See Hobog. Art. B.)*

When therefore a rational ontological requirement excludes the concept of a Sophianic "lineage" of Buddhas, it is their own "personage" that is Sophianized—that is, experienced as the achievement of the working of Prajñā-Sophia—which is to say saving the liberators and causing them to be born into the Knowledge that saves. No doubt, most often these figures get commented on as metaphors or personifications. As for the personifications, it makes sense to accompany Jung in contemplating this point: the symbols they represent are in no way arbitrary constructions erected rationally and after the fact but rather active *ab initio* persons who are directing the whole effort of the imagination that *a priori* informs the mental vision.

CONCLUSION: THE SELF AND SOPHIA

Because the Buddhas have never had any resemblance to Yahweh, there has never been a need for an *Answer to Job*. Therefore, the blossoming of Buddhist Sophiology does not correspond to that kind of need. It is of critical importance to note that the Sophianic aspect of the Buddhas and Bodhisattvas is structured according to the individuation of their appearance to beings, to the epiphanies of their *corpus spirituale*. Therefore, we need to mention the characteristic trait of our apocryphal Christians in which Christ appeared to each disciple, man or woman, according to the personal form or the individual Image that corresponded to his or her soul and according to the extent of his or her unformulated expectation or incessant desire. *(Note to be written concerning* Talem eum vidi qualem capere potui.*)* This individuation of the Vision sets up a relationship that is both personal and specific. It is the deepest meaning that the figure of the angel can reveal—this angel whose traits also indicate certain resemblances to those of the Bodhisattvas. Everywhere we have discovered its traces, the representation of Sophia as found in Sophiology and in the experience of its figures and its relationships seems to us to be unified with the concept and process of individuation. This amounts to a remarkable confirmation of this Sophiology, which Jung was led to recognize and formulate through a long experimental path. Based on this fact, it makes it possible for us to specify why Buddhism is not monotheism, or polytheism, or atheism, or pantheism. If a term were really needed, perhaps we would have to say kathenotheism. From the individual totality blossoming in this way each time, the mandala remains the unifying symbol both as a means of expression and as mental attainment.

One other and final consequence is raised by the mention of such a symbol. It concerns this notion, this nature of the Self that, in the interpretation of Jung's thought, can cause considerable confusion and raise questions that are sometimes fertile and sometimes pointless. Let us begin with this double premise: that Jung repudiates all agnosticism and all skepticism with respect to powers that are higher than man, but at the same time he recognizes a valid and sensible affirmation only within the limits of an "experimental metaphysics." *Answer to Job* would indicate then the exact scope of an assertion such as this: the Image of God is an archetype of the Self. It is possible for me to recognize as real only that which, in one way or another, in one sense or another, acts on me (the powerlessness of all argumentation based on reason to produce a conviction in the soul and in the heart as well as in the intellect). Admitting the possibility of this action as a postulate, does it remain to be seen whether we can distinguish that the angel who is present to the soul comes from God or from the depths of the Unconscious? In fact, posed in this way the question is not at an appropriate level. What reveals and indicates the central symbols of the process of individuation is the Self, about which we can repeat along with the alchemists *Habet mille nomina*. From this it follows that it is not with the Unconscious, the transconsciousness pure and simple, that the Image of God coincides with in any case. Rather it is with one of its specific contents; namely, an archetype, which we clearly cannot then separate from this Image. This is already enough to challenge the premises of any religious phenomenology that claims to pose as a dilemma, on one and the same level, the indeterminate Self and the figure of the God of scriptural monotheism.

We must think and hold conjointly here (in the thought) the idea of the Self and that of the archetype. The Self represents the totality and as such, as well as individual totality, it is transcendent to consciousness and can be experienced only partially. This is what Jung means by proposing it as a maximal concept, comparable to Kant's "thing-in-itself"—a postulate that justifies itself and motivates itself psychologically but cannot be demonstrated scientifically. *(Compare G.F. 135 and Psy. Al. 263.)* On the other hand, when we speak of the archetype of the Self, we need to think specifically of the Greek word *typos,* which has the meaning of a minting (of a coin) or an imprint (as in printing). The idea of archetype connotes something that strikes and impresses. Whereas the religious point of view (shall we say rather theological) conceives of the typos as being the effect and the form itself of the imprint . . .

PART II

ANSWER TO JOB

Mrs. Corbin insistently requested that I bring together the two texts that her husband had written on Jung's *Answer to Job*. The first, "Eternal Sophia," had already appeared twice: first in the *Revue de culture européenne,* in 1953, and then in the *Cahier de L'Herne,* which was devoted to Jung, in 1984. The second text formed a postscript to the publication by Buchet-Chastel of the French-language translation of Jung's book by Roland Cahen. I am reproducing here therefore these two texts exactly as they were given to me.

MICHEL CAZENAVE

1

ETERNAL SOPHIA*

The present article was written twenty years ago and published in the no-longer-extant Revue de Culture européenne.† *This is a sufficient stretch of time to warrant a modification of the state and aspect of the research. It is likely that, if we were to write the article again today, we might extend it with further commentary. In particular the work of Gershom Scholem has led us to become acquainted with certain aspects of Jewish mysticism based on which we might be able to outline a different* Answer to Job *that is equally Sophianic but with a traditional resonance.*

In its present form this article had the approval of the late C. G. Jung and was the starting point of long and friendly discussions on all the points raised about the book. As everyone knows, Answer to Job‡ *provoked a great tumult of hostile critique from all quarters. This is why the article is reproduced here just as it appeared at the time, because*

---

*This text in italics reproduces Henry Corbin's original. We can see clearly how it was at that time an introduction to his participation in the book *Sophia Æterna*—a book that was never published and that is to be found evoked in the appendices—and how this manuscript was subsequently picked up again and revised by the author. —*Ed.*
†*Revue de Culture européenne* 3, first trimester (1953).
‡C. G. Jung, *Antwort auf Hiob* (Zürich: Rascher Verlag, 1952).

as such it belongs to the history of Jungian thought and the echoes that his thought encountered during his lifetime. The references provided in the notes correspond to the state of the bibliography of that time. Since then, translations have been done, and Jung's body of work is better known in France, but of course our references to the original German text have been maintained here because that was a necessary condition so as to ensure the homogeneity of our analysis. (Answer to Job was later translated into French under the care of Dr. Roland Cahen.) As for the theological allusions, notably the allusion to the Sophiology of Father Sergei Bulgakov, they were later the topic of conversations with C. G. Jung.

Our article takes its point of departure from an interview conducted by Mircea Eliade. The text of this interview appears elsewhere in this volume.* I was happy to be able to add my own account to that of Mircea Eliade concerning the annual meetings of the Eranos Circle at Ascona, and I am happy to reconfirm that happiness today. The Eranos Jahrbuch *[Eranos yearbook] is now at its fortieth volume. The considerable work that is included there belongs henceforth to the history of our times. We are grateful for the opportunity given us to recall that here.*

1973

I

Upon the occasion of the interview conducted a few months ago by Mircea Eliade,† Professor C. G. Jung retraced the stages of his long spiritual itinerary, *longissima via.* For the first time, he expressed directly in French the teaching that emerges from many years of study devoted to alchemical texts. Alchemy was from then on no longer

---

*Reference here is to the unpublished volume *Sophia Æterna.*
†See the issue of *Combat* for Thursday, October 9, 1952.

understood by Jung to be some kind of "pre-chemistry" or an "experimental science" still clinging to the excuse of being embryonic—but rather a spiritual technique the operations of which were quite *real,* certainly, but a reality that is not that of pure and simple physics. Not yet translated, this part of Jung's body of work remains perhaps closed to many readers. Not only does the work already stretch over several volumes, but, in relation to earlier work, it announces a characteristic discovery in relation to the body of work thought or published by Jung in the course of about the past fifteen years.* Any allusion to this work, as a whole, would be henceforth irrelevant, if we were not able to take account of this valorization of the symbolism of alchemy, the reasoning in his methods, and the results of this analysis.

Even though applying a different method, Mircea Eliade had arrived, for his part, at convergent results in studying the operations of Chinese and Indian alchemists. Quite rightly, he saw in this convergence a "stunning confirmation of Jung's hypothesis." And we can take from that as well how that convergence is a symbol of those memorable meetings for which each summer for twenty years the Eranos Circle at Ascona has been the mystical gathering place. Eliade opportunely mentions the role of these meetings, the success of which is due to the enthusiastic initiative and unfailing willingness of Mrs. Olga Fröbe-Kapteyn. The community that comes together each session, including scholars—each of whom is at the forefront of his discipline and all of whom as well are the most individualistic beings in the world—is already something like a miracle of Spirit and Mind. Each person participating in these sessions, organized each time around a given theme, can bear witness to what he has received. Jung's presence there occasioned contacts that would never have been possible outside of this

---

*Compare notably *Paracelsica* (Zürich: Rascher Verlag, 1942); *Psychologie und Alchemie,* 1944; *Die Psychologie der Übertragung, Erläutert anhand einer alchemistischen Bilderserie,* (Zürich: Rascher Verlag, 1946); *Symbolik des Geistes,* 1948, and so on.

absolute spiritual freedom in which each person held forth without any concern for official dogma while trying to be none other than himself, and truthful.

It is under these conditions, and these conditions alone, that an encounter with Jung's work and thought can, indeed, produce fertile results. And it is in this spirit that his books must be read; otherwise the reading will invalidate the book's perspective. Jung's *Antwort auf Hiob* (*Answer to Job*) is addressed to the individual, to the man capable of thinking loyally, in private, face to face with himself. Because this book is itself a work of the most authentic individuality. *Monos pros monon.* This passionate book is the confession of an entire life, and the perspective that it opens is precisely that of the lively unfolding that is announced by the mystery of alchemy deeply examined as a mystery of the soul's deliverance.

That the alchemical mystery is, in this sense, the mystery of Wisdom or eternal Sophia, that the real accomplishment of its rites accompanies the birth of the *homo totus* (*Ars totum requirit hominem*) in the innermost recesses of the person of the adept, and that this whole comes about through the conjunction of one's earthly "I" with that of one's celestial soul, one's *Anima caelestis,* the Virgo Sophia—all of that a practitioner of the theosophy of Jakob Böhme can already know. But what is new is that it is no longer a question of some adherence to a doctrine exemplified in a limited case or by a leap forward of sympathy that draws its motivation only from within itself. What is new is the analysis that sends light into the depths and discovers, under all the exemplifications of the archetype, the constancy of the motivations. This is the soul placed in the presence of what is coming about in it *when* that takes place and *so that* when that takes place the figure of Sophia appears on its horizon; and then it is capable of achieving the individuation that this figure proposes and anticipates as a living and liberating symbol.

It is customary to specify when one mentions, for example, the procession of hypostases of Avicennian Neoplatonism, that it is a matter of an ontological succession and not a chronological one. It is in this same sense that it would seem that in contrast to Hegel's phenomenology, we can say that Jung's phenomenology continually begins with the prehistory of the soul, because this prehistory is not enclosed in the past and shut away with the past. It is always imminent. Once and for all it is not fixed at a period in the chronology from which its inheritance is transmitted. Each time it is "at the beginning" and attests to itself through the recurrence of archetypes. He who would try to sketch the phases of the Sophianic religion across the religious climates that geographic distances separate—but which in the singular Soul are nearby—such a one finds himself then, with the last book of Jung's, imposing new tasks and also proposing new help. For this book outlines a really extraordinary phenomenology of the Sophianic religion. He does this, not at all by conforming to the classic plan of the "history of salvation" (Heilsgeschichte) that is always recopied by the traditional Christian theologians. Instead it is done in an entirely novel fashion, with the daring of one who knows that authority derives only from the personal experience of an entire lifetime. About the question of Job remaining without answer at the annunciation of the reign of eternal Sophia, magnifying in an unexpected theological sense the recent pontifical proclamation about the dogma of the Assumption of the Virgin Mary, there is now established an unprecedented phenomenology. This book contains all that is needed to provoke "scandal," drawing upon itself all the rigors of both the Catholic and Protestant camps.*

---

*Contrast this with the positive article published by the theologian Hans Reverend Schär, "C. G. Jung und die Deutung der Geschichte," in *Schweizerische Theologische Umschau* (July 1952): 91. We owe as well a debt to Reverend Schär for the excellent book *Religion und Seele in der Psychologie C. G. Jungs* (Zürich: Rascher Verlag, 1946).

The author is *alone,* strong with the force of his soul alone. In our times, such a case is already extraordinary and calls for a singular respect. He is not the spokesman of any religious faith, any dogma, or any institution. There is a treacherous little expression that is intended to ruin the credibility of the person at whom it is targeted: "Such a person represents only himself." In contrast, the meaning here in this case would be precisely what conveys all the grandeur, all the force, and all the authenticity. For how many men today could claim really to be "representatives" of themselves, when they represent only collective norms, official dogmas, and ready-made opinions? It is because we are in the presence here of this man alone that I would like to invite all those alone to contemplate this book, to listen to this message, if really they are alone. The authentic totality cannot be born here except from the solitudes and in solitude. The theology we have here is not learned in manuals or through the historical critique of texts, but in the night and the suffering of the soul, in the sacred struggle that is engaged innerly without compromise, without cowardice, and without abdication. It corresponds to the ideal case of this individual religion that the theologian Schleiermacher tried with such fervor to describe. It is not impossible that one day he will become once again very contemporary. Only the person whose central personal intuition allows the whole religious edifice to be connected to this central intuition can establish himself at the heart of any given religious form. Only such a person really has "the keys to the city in the religious world." It is in a perfectly monadologist spirit, inspired by Leibniz, that the great Romantic theologian, having no conception of a possible incarnation without individuation, and appreciating the case of the person who, with his own given religious form, cannot adapt to those that already exist—wrote, "He who would not be able to construct it himself, if it had not already existed, such a person will not connect himself either to one of the existing [religions] but will be constrained to produce a new one in himself."*

It is not by chance that along with the name of Schleiermacher, the terms *individuation* and *incarnation* find themselves conjoined here. It is toward this conjunction that we will make our way finally in the following pages. Certainly, C. G. Jung intends to speak only in his capacity as a psychologist and to pursue only psychology. He denies being a theologian or even a philosopher of religion. But were we to say "nothing but a psychologist, nothing but psychology," suddenly we would have the feeling of having committed a grave injustice, of having put oneself, in a manner of speaking, in the same camp as all those who, frightened for one reason or another by the scope of Jung's works, conclude after each new scope of this kind, "This is only psychology." However, we are entitled then to wonder what have they done with their soul, with their psyche, as if they had sent these parts on holiday so they could then dare to relegate them to "It's only that." Why is it necessary then that as soon as it is shown that there are certain factors in the psyche that correspond to divine figures, certain people shout blasphemy as if all was lost and these figures were devalued?†

To what depreciation must the soul, the psyche, be submitted in order to make of it only "nature" or "natural?" And what depreciation must there be so that the fact of speaking of the reality of the soul and of the soul as a reality is immediately labeled with the reproach

---

*Schleiermacher, *Discours sur la religion,* translated by I. J. Rouge (Paris: Éditions Aubier-Montaigne, 1944), 290. I have quoted from the edition of 1806; other editions water down the force of this passage. It is worth the trouble to continue a few lines further in the quotation, because of the extent to which it formulates the most intrepid profession of "monadological" faith, with the conviction that the microcosm of the personal individual is a whole cosmos. "If he remains alone with his religion, without disciples, no damage will be done. Always and everywhere there exist seeds of what cannot yet attain a more widespread existence; they nonetheless exist and the religion I am speaking about exists as well. It has just as well a face and a given organization. It is just as much a positive religion as if he had founded a great school."

†Compare this with *Psychologie und Alchemie* (Zürich: Rascher Verlag, 1944), 21.

of "psychologizing"? It is both a grave misunderstanding and such a childish game that Jung himself, taking the initiative, compares "psychologizing" to a kind of magico-primitive thinking. (You're still there? Unheard of! Get out of here! You have been explained away.)* It is quite necessary to tell oneself however that a theory in physics that tries to explain light does not thereby suppress the light. Religious images and statements are not subject to our power. These are psychic events that reveal themselves to the inner experience as if charged with such an extraordinary *numinosity* that the numinosity portrays them as different from their transcendent object. Statements and images do not *position* their transcendent object (as the reproach of psychologizing would have it); they interpret it.

With respect to Jungians, the reproach of psychologizing alternates with the contrary reproach that charges them with creating a neo-gnostic metaphysics, a reestablishment of Neoplatonic hypostases.† These are contradictory reproaches that cancel each other out and give rise to the suspicion of their having been promulgated by people who no doubt had something other than their soul to save, something heavy and weighty that is not being admitted. If, precisely, psychology is *nothing but* that (*nur Psychologie!*), but instead all of that—that is, the Science and Consciousness of this soul without which man would be only Nature—then, in his turn, the seeker who is not professionally a psychologist but something of a philosopher of religion—let us say in order to simplify things a "hierologist"‡—will feel directly interested by

---

*Jung, *Antwort auf Hiob*, 159; compare with pages 5–11 and 158.

†Which have no need of being reestablished, since they have never been abolished except in mental universes not capable of understanding them.

‡Let us pause here to express regret that we must always have recourse in French to the circumlocution *science des religions* (science of religion), which is not moreover a *histoire des religions* (history of religion). The simple term *hierology* (proposed formerly by Goblet d'Alviella) would have been a simple way of designating the *science du sacré* (science of the sacred).

Jung's research to the extent that this research renews the whole study of symbols and symbolism. Not that there is any need to draw conclusions or alter them in one direction or another. It is a meditation that must be practiced here in unison with a work developing out to far horizons, which a long human life is daring to peek into. Meditate with the author, not to repeat what he is doing but to arrive at oneself, without any fear of walking alone if need be. Here it is no longer a question of polemics, and the science is no longer a simple matter of erudition—it is integrated with the absolutely personal destiny of the seeker.

Answer to Job rings like strange reminder of religious topics that, about twenty years ago, were food for certain young philosopher-theologians questing for a new horizon that would be truly their own. Strange reminder. Each one of those individuals can indeed measure the path that was traveled since then in his own search, and then the hypothesis is double. Perhaps one group of them will find formulated differently in this book what they in any case foresaw—that toward which they were beating a path and are continuing to beat a path. And perhaps others, established along the way in some solid resting place, will refuse to take on the adventure of picking up once again the quest of their youth. There was then—to name only two of the voices—the voice of Kierkegaard, the "Christian Job," who attracted young Protestant philosophers in the adventure of subjectivity as truth;* and it is perhaps the triumph of a piece of humor that Kierkegaard tasted when the theology of subjectivity transformed in their successors into a dogmatic theology with impermeable ramparts. And there was the voice of Father Sergei Bulgakov, herald of Sophia and of Sophianic thought, who, along with Nikolai Berdyaev, rediscovered the secrets of a tradition that at least had

---

*Let us recall the group "Hic et nunc," around the years 1931–1933: Denis de Rougemont, Albert-Marie Schmidt, Roland de Pury, plus Roger Jézéquel and the signatory of these pages.

been neglected for all those whose thought was connected in one way or another with Russian Orthodoxy.

Those who will have heard this voice, then or since then, will be no doubt the most accepting of this "Sophianic" book of C. G. Jung, and it will at least not be an object of scandal for them. The confrontation requires a whole book. Indicating that here simply will be one of the conclusions of these few pages, which also would like to suggest how this same book, which in itself is no longer simply psychology but rather falls under the rubric of prophetic philosophy, can stimulate fertile contemplation in the seeker who, professionally, finds himself not simply in contact but in a state of needing to understand *ab intra* religious domains outside of Christianity.

II

We need therefore to point out the major structures of *Answer to Job,* the three grand acts of a divine drama of which the story of Job will be the point of departure. We need to specify here the reading conditions that will not distort either the tone or the intention of the book. A first condition would be that we give up opposing it by "sticking" historical exegesis and criticism onto it; to do so would be ridiculously pedantic (there are always people, it is true, for whom the cure must not be gotten without following the rules, even if such people don't taste, above all, the consolation of knowing the ill person was cured but instead died). Then, if you please, for the reasons mentioned earlier, we must not give in to the old habit of incriminating with "psychologizing" anyone who refers to the experience of the *soul,* which includes just as much the "psychic" as the "spiritual" (unless someone can tell us what would be for the human being another place or location for this experience, or, dispensing with that, unless someone can tell us what divine figures or theological propositions have still a meaning and for whom). It is not just simply a provisional or negative attitude that is required here. It is an affirmation of the primacy of the soul that C. G. Jung solemnly reminds us about at the beginning of his book.

There are experiences, events, and truths that are physical; and there are experiences, events, and truths that are psychic. The confusion between one and the other and the inability to recognize the autonomy of the second triad is the greatest calamity that can befall a consciousness, not to mention a whole "spiritual" culture. Has it always and everywhere been this way—that a thing is not recognized as true unless its reality is presented or conceived of as physical? This "naturalization" has reached such a point that if one denies the physical reality of a historical fact, it seems that one makes everything tumble down, whereas it ought to be just the opposite: degrading the misunderstood facts and reality of the Spirit, of the Mind to the level of events having a physical sense, inserting physical events into the web of history—that is what ought to be experienced as the crumbling of our faith and of our hope. Many blasphemies, conscious and unconscious, would never have been spoken concerning the fact of the virginal conception of Christ if Christianity had not been prey to this inability.*

And that is the reason why the touching pages devoted by Jung to the dogma of the Assumption of Mary (accepted in its literal truth, which, specifically as such, is not a physical truth) will be appreciated only with difficulty by that one of the churches that most especially ought to be happy with it.

Now, the question that the book of Job is going to pose will not be that of knowing how the men of the Old Testament experienced the reality of their God, how there was revealed to them the contra-

---

*It is known that in Islam as well there is a very ancient theological debate in which the issue is knowing if the Ascension that the Prophet was granted is to be understood as a spiritual ascension or an ascension *in corpore*.

dictory Image of a God excessive in his emotions and in his fury, suffering from this excess and confessing that wrath and jealousy were devouring him. Rather it is a question of knowing how a man of our times, a man of Christian culture and education, can find himself confronted with and by the Divine Darkness that appears in the book of Job, and how it acts on him, on the condition that it is understood that the most open acceptance of the irrational is not confused in any way with an abdication when faced with the absurd. Necessarily, the phenomenology must follow here the unfolding of a divine drama, the experience of which stretches the whole length of a story. What must never be forgotten is that the phenomenon is never like this except for the consciousness in which it is revealed. Yahweh, in *his own* being can be unveiled only *in* and *to* the consciousness of the religious man whose mode of being was faith in Yahweh. And, in its turn, it is this appearing, as a phenomenon of the second degree, that is reflected here in the phenomenology of Job for the Consciousness of modern man; it is the only event on which phenomenology is really set. Already, putting this in parentheses ought to be enough for the naive Consciousness to save itself, if need be, any pious indignation that puts the Consciousness beyond itself. If it were so, the naive Consciousness would place its object as outside itself, in the contradictory status of a thing not revealed that would be revealed to it, or of a revealed thing, a *phainomenon,* that would not be revealed.

1. The Absence of Sophia

The phases of the psychic Event such as it appears in Jung's analysis cannot be taken up here in all the details of their sequence; we will try however to follow them step by step. I have spoken above of the three grand acts of a sacred drama. Taking in fact as an ongoing topic the increasing precision of the Sophianic vision, a triple Event seems to me to punctuate the sequencing. A first act, filled with bursts of wrath from Yahweh, is characterized by the absence of Sophia, of whom there is only a presentiment. A second act announces her return "to the present" for the consciousness and for the divine anthropomorphosis. The third act is that of her Exaltation.

The first act is dominated by the constant and final attitude of Job as seen in his response, "I am a too little thing; what am I to answer? I put my hand upon my mouth."* Job knows that he is in front of a superhuman being, a God who has no concern for any moral judgment or any ethical obligation. But he also knows that God, just because of that, finds himself in such total contradiction with himself, that Job is certain to find in God a support against God. (Kierkegaard also said something similar: The pious man is not he who, once and for all, recognizes himself as guilty before God, but he who, like Job, struggles *for* God *against* God.) For Job knows that, from now on, a witness, an advocate lives for him in Heaven: "I know that my avenger lives; a defender will rise up for me out of the dust."† But this helpful defender, this avenger who will bring about change that penetrates right to Yahweh's essence, has not yet revealed his name.

How did this internal divine antinomy come to burst forth? The jealous and irritable essence of Yahweh demands a personal rapport with man; he is drawn to man, and that is what differentiates his personal essence from the figure of Zeus, for example. Now this demand has provided itself with the guarantee of a contract, to be played out in one direction or another, according to whether men behaved as Yahweh desired and expected. Incredible event: Yahweh broke his contract. More incredible still is the origin of this break. Certainly it is not the irreproachable faithfulness of his servant Job. It is rather the thought of

---

*Job 40:4; Jung, *Antwort auf Hiob*, 39, 37.
†Job 19:25; Jung, *Antwort auf Hiob*, 18.

a doubt about this faithfulness, a doubt about which Yahweh's omniscience could have preserved him but which nevertheless is actually the *son* of this thought, and it is called Satan, "one of his sons." And this son influences him with an astonishing ease. Why should that have to turn into a wager falling on the back of the poor and powerless human creature? And that God should deliver his servant to the bad Spirit, so that Job is thrown into the abyss, while God permits the violation of at least three of the commandments given by himself on Mount Sinai.

We will mention in ending this section the Iranian tradition that considers Ahriman as the Son of Darkness, engendered by a doubt of Zurvan, eternal Time. Even here, this thought of doubt, this Darkness, seems to reach the gravity that it assumes in Iranian Zurvanism—because poor Job is struck down, out of the running. However, the emphatic insistence of Yahweh on his all-powerfulness seems to be targeting a listener who would still have some doubt on this point. In fact, it is himself whom Yahweh is thinking about, not Job, but this thought of doubt that is his son Satan. And when Satan loses his wager, there is in Yahweh's consciousness the dark presentiment of something that threatens his all-powerfulness. He addresses himself to Job, who has been struck down for a long time, in terms such as these, "I want to question you; you Job, instruct me."* Is this not challenging Job as if he were not simply a "valiant man" but a God? Now that is possible only because Yahweh projects on Job the face of a doubter whom he doesn't like because he is Yahweh's own (Yahweh's doubt about his own faithfulness), a face that considers him with an unsettling critical regard.†

A new fact has in effect intervened—Job has learned to know God: "My ear had heard talk of you, but now my eye has seen you.

---

*Job 40:7.
†Job 19:25; compare with Jung, *Antwort auf Hiob,* 32–35, 48.

This is why I condemn myself and repent in dust and ashes."* A response that is clear and yet ambiguous. Job had been naïve—he had imagined an alliance, perhaps a "Good God," but now he has seen with horror that Yahweh is *nothing human,* and even in this sense, less than a man; he is what he himself says of the crocodile: "His heart is hard as stone [. . .] All that grows trembles before him. He is the king of the proudest animals."† But in not letting himself be diverted from presenting his case to God, even though without hope or fulfillment, he has created this obstacle on which Yahweh's essence will have to manifest, just as a mortal through his moral attitude can even without knowing it be raised to the stars from where he will be looking into "the back of the divine."‡

"Where were you when I founded the earth? Tell me if you have the intelligence."§ The only response that Job receives is that of a brutal demiurge, crushing man with his superiority: "I am not submitted to any ethical law. I am the Creator of indomitable and pitiless natural forces."¶ But if the divine unconscious makes possible the conception that removes divine action from all moral judgment, would that be *the* response to Job, or mustn't this response come from elsewhere? For the material "reparations" that provide a "happy ending" to the drama, leave the question totally intact. Yahweh wants to be loved, adored, praised for his justice, and he behaves like a natural catastrophe. The curtain falls on the story of Job, but an unheard-of scandal is immanent in metaphysics, and no one has a formula ready that could save the monotheistic concept of divinity from catastrophe. The drama has been played for all of eternity. Yahweh's double nature has become

---

*Job 42:5.
†Job 41:24–25, 41:34.
‡Jung, *Antwort auf Hiob,* 30, 36–39.
§Job 38:4.
¶I cannot find any verse in Job corresponding to this quotation. —*Trans.*

manifest. "Such a revelation, whether or not it penetrates into the consciousness of men, cannot remain without consequence."*

2. Sophia's Anamnesis

The curtain has fallen once again on Job's silence. "I put my hand on my mouth; I have spoken once; I will no longer respond."† And this silence is heavy with an unsatisfactory question.

From the abyss of this silence of threatening potentialities, a new voice emerges as if from an eternal, forgotten past. The second act of the divine drama that Jung's book describes begins with the first intervention of this voice.‡ Because this voice resonates like that of the witness, the advocate who has been invoked, "I know that from now on there lives in Heaven a witness in my favor."§ It's not a matter here related to a problem of literary history, nor is it a matter of determining the chronology of the writing of wisdom texts in relation to the chronology of the Book of Job. It is a matter of the destiny of Yahweh as it is present for the human being, from preconscious depths, and it is a matter of the metamorphosis that is preparing for the annunciation of she whose reign will give Job his answer: "The idea of Sophia or divine wisdom (*Sapientia Dei*), a Spirit (*Pneuma*) of *a feminine nature*—we could say a coeternal hypostasis existing before Creation." At this point the author gathers together and amplifies the most beautiful texts that form something like an Old Testament of the Sophianic religion.

Proverbs: "I have been established for eternity, from the beginning, before the Earth's beginning [. . .] When the Eternal placed the foundation of the Earth, I was working beside him and every day

---

*Jung, *Antwort auf Hiob*, 42.
†Job 40:5.
‡Jung, *Antwort auf Hiob*, 43ff.
§Job 19:25.

I made his delights [. . .] and finding my happiness among the children of men [. . .] He who finds me has found life."* The Book of Sirach: "I have come from the mouth of the Most High [. . .] I am the mother of noble love.† The Wisdom of Solomon, in which Sophia's spiritual nature is affirmed, as a shaper of worlds, as a friend of human beings sent from the Throne of Grandeur, and as a Holy Spirit, as a psychopomp leading to God and guaranteeing immortality. This Old Testament would not be complete until it is reunited across all of man's presentiments, across all the witnessing of an eternal Sophianic religion, for the biblical Sophia is not only the symptom of a Greek influence. Jung knew this, and his reference to Indian *Shakti*‡ is an allusion to a whole ensemble (gnosis, Manichaeism, alchemy, and so on), the meaning of which his own studies progressively made clear and which today bursts forth in the "personage" of Sophia.

How is it that in the wisdom books, God seems to be remembering once again this eternal feminine companion who is providing no less for his delight than she is for the delight of men? If there has been forgetting, the hard necessity that motivated this anamnesis, this recalling "to the present" appears in the fact that Job knew God, no longer by hearsay but with his own eyes. Yahweh's antinomic nature was not able to be divulged and it remained hidden and unconscious only to himself. "He who knows God, acts upon God. The failure of the attempt to corrupt Job changed Yahweh . . ."§

Sophia's absence is manifested in Yahweh's strange behavior. Blame and disapproval are never inflicted on Satan; there is almost a complicity in the facility with which Job is abandoned to him. Satan is a little too interested in men—his interventions provoke complications and

---

*Proverbs 8:23, 8:30–31, 8:35.

†Book of Sirach, 24:3.

‡Jung, *Antwort auf Hiob*, 44.

§Jung, *Antwort auf Hiob*, 49.

extravagances that were not foreseen in the initial plan of Creation. They will lead to a necessity for draconian punishment (the Flood). In all that, Yahweh is continually looking for a cause not at all in one of his sons called Satan, but in the victims—the human beings. This behavior developed in human beings a "religion of fear" whose traces are found even in the wisdom books, since it is said there that "Fear of God is the beginning of wisdom,"* whereas this fear is not something that Sophia could have created. It is the absence and forgetting of Sophia that denounces the formation of this patriarchal society,† a society with a preponderance of males, where the woman has only secondary significance, and where the subjugation of feminine human being implies contempt for and forgetting of all Sophianic "values" and feelings. Correlatively, for Yahweh, forgetful of the eternal coexistence of Sophia, there is then substituted the alliance with the "chosen people," constrained to the feminine role of Yahweh's wife but precisely according to the rules of patriarchal society. Fear and trembling. Absence of Eros. Yahweh has no regard for man, but instead for an aim in which man must serve him as an auxiliary.

In this critical development, Job will have marked a culminating point. He will have been the herald of dangerous thought, of the requirement that calls on the wisdom of Gods and men without even having yet a clear knowledge of Sophia. "Because men feel exposed to divine arbitrariness, they need Sophia, unlike Yahweh for whom until now nothing is opposed except man's nothingness."‡ And because Job had seen this face of God, men of the final pre-Christian centuries achieved the anamnesis of the preexisting Sophia. Her light touch compensates for Yahweh and his attitude. It shows human beings the only luminous and tender, kindly and just aspect of their God. The

---

*Proverbs 9:10.

†Jung, *Antwort auf Hiob*, 54ff.

‡Jung, *Antwort auf Hiob*, 57.

reappearance of Sophia announces a totally new future. Her demiurgic activity makes divine thoughts real; she gives them material form and structure, which is the prerogative of feminine being. It is from her coexistence, from her eternal *hieros gamos* with Yahweh that worlds are engendered. Job saw with terror that there was nothing human about Yahweh. The imminent change is this: God wants to renew himself in the mysteries of celestial hierogamy, and wants to become man.

Already we are at the heart of Jung's most personal exegesis. It will attain a tone of emotion in which we perceive the passion contained in a soul for whom none of the interpretations that are ready-made, frozen, and venerated in the framework of secular traditions could be an insurmountable obstacle, preventing the attainment of the ultimate and inexorable truth of facing alone the *self of one's self.* In the following pages,* there is the secret vibration of a Sophianic hymn, hailing the approach of the eternal Virgin, which means a new creation—not the creation of a new world, but the creation of a new God.

God wants to change his own essence. It is not new men who must be created but rather a single God-Man. And the great overturning will be accomplished: the second Adam is not to emerge immediately and directly from the hands of the creator; he must be engendered by the feminine human being. This is not only in the sense of an event in time but in a substantial meaning in which the primacy falls to a second Eve. Just as Adam is equivalent to the original androgyne, so too "woman and her posterity" is equivalent to a human couple: the *Regina caelestis* and divine mother, and the divine son who has no human father. The Event announces the independence and autonomy of the Virgin Mother with respect to man, the male. She is a daughter of God. Rejecting this Event as a simple dogmatic definition of the privilege of the *Conceptio immaculate* that exempts the Virgin Mother

---

*Jung, *Antwort auf Hiob,* 59ff.

from the stain of "original sin" is to not see where this Event is situated. The Virgin Mother carries not only the *imago Dei;* as divine bride she incarnates its prototype—Sophia. In the Old Testament* and through this archetypal relationship she is much more, in her being and in her role, than the earthly agent of the Incarnation.

We will find these correspondences and typifications also in the Sophiology of Father Bulgakov. No doubt they are nuanced by a different theological context, a more traditional one, but one in which the Tradition contains what elsewhere has been allowed to fall away if not be intentionally rejected. It is true here that certain demanding consequences will come to light and they will be joined by those of other traditions. Their validity, measured by their psycho-spiritual reality, does not depend on any dogmatic directorship. For the *Conceptio immaculate* means *status ante lapsum,* the state before the fall, and this implies that she who had that privilege escapes the general condition of humanity. She comes to signify once again "a paradisiacal, pleromatic, and divine existence." The Virgin Mother is raised, we might say, to the condition of a goddess and sheds her humanity. She will not conceive her Child in sin as all other mothers, because this Child also will be a God, and a God cannot be conceived in sin. "Both, Mother and Son, are not really human beings, but Gods."†

Jung wonders if it has ever been really considered that the divine incarnation was, because of just that, brought into question, or at least partially reduced and attenuated. In response, the theologies and the theologians would have quantities of things to distinguish and to remark on, all more or less convincing and all accommodating more or less well the essentials. For it is certain that the formulation above drives the psychic Event to an extreme consequence, as it was driven

---

*Jung, *Antwort auf Hiob,* 60.
†Jung, *Antwort auf Hiob,* 61.

uncompromisingly also by those schools that we bunch together under the denomination of "docetist" so as to cast them into oblivion as "heresies," simple objects of curiosity for "historians of ideas." And yet there is an eternal Docetism, archetypical if you prefer, of which the phenomenology remains to be undertaken. From this point of view, the old "heresies" have much to teach us. Clinging to the temporal, we lose our footing as soon as the identity between the *historical* Event and the *chronological* and *physical* reality is brought into question. What we are passionately attempting to "save" differs here and there. Doubtless the concepts of divine anthropomorphosis and incarnation (*ensarkōsis*) have several ways of being associated and disassociated, and a "docetist" could judge the idea and the event of the Incarnation as being definitively compromised by the concept formulated by official Christianity. In any case, this exaltation of the Virgin Mother and the Son has a lengthy past. It would be appropriate to mention here all that could be contemplated on the topic of *Christos-angelos,* but also the representation of the Virgin Mother as an angel who would have been sent ahead to the Earth by the Father.* In this form once again there is expressed the "celestial" unity of the Mother and the Son, incarnating respectively Sophia and Logos, both "project managers" of Creation.

It is normal that here we run into concepts of history and of historicity, meaning the difficulty—at least for the profane understanding of our times—of considering the eternal Event and the historical Event to be identical. We need to be comfortable with the idea of a unique historical Event already accomplished in eternity and with the idea that historical Time is a relative concept that must be rounded out by a concept of a simultaneous existence in Heaven or in the ple-

---

*Compare this with Henri-Charles Puech and André Vaillant, *Le Traité contre les Bogomiles de Cosmas le prêtre* [The treaty against Bogomil Cosmas the priest] (Paris: Imprimerie Nationale, 1945), 207.

roma. Jung reminds us opportunely of all these problems.* At this point there appears, along with the idea of a plane of historical continuity, or a plane of recurrence of archetypes, a new way of considering the meaning of *prefigurations,* and along with them the foundation of this typological exegesis, the usage of which is so abusive when it treats figures as if they were things.

Also at this point there arises an indication that, based on the case of Job, there is some point in wondering about the real motivation for the Incarnation as an historical event. We must insist on this point because it was in fact this motivation that caused some individuals who were prey to an exaggerated sense of humor to say that Jung had "psychoanalyzed Yahweh." We had to remind readers at the beginning that, if, phenomenologically, we are to speak of the "states of consciousness of Yahweh," it is only insofar as Yahweh has revealed himself and is knowable in the awareness or unconscious depths of those whose faith has revealed him in this way; it is there that these variations are graspable and "analyzable," and it is there, in their turn, that these contents and meanings can be reflected upon—and they do need to be—in the consciousness of others, such as in that of an analytical psychologist. Without the possibility of these reappearances and intercommunications we wouldn't ever have anything to talk about. We can then discern for example† that up until Sophia's appearance, Yahweh's mode of action is presented and is experienced as if accompanied by a mode of consciousness that is quite inferior—"purely perceptive consciousness." But we know that, in this case, acts of thought take place in the depths, from which they emerge in dreams, visions, or revelations—sudden changes in consciousness. The episode of Job gave rise to something like that. The superiority of Job, crushed by

---

*Jung, *Antwort auf Hiob,* 64ff.
†Jung, *Antwort auf Hiob,* 69ff.

defeat, rises up into "Yahweh's consciousness." In a delayed reaction, the Creator experiences himself through his creature. He has to catch up with him. Note Sophia's merciful intervention here and the awareness of this delay—a delay that can only be overcome by God *becoming man* (here we are on the path toward a reversal of the traditional conception of the Incarnation). The historical Event will exemplify, will render historical the eternal archetype—Abel's destiny—but also the God dying in the flower of youth from the pre-Christian religions. It is no longer a question of a national Messiah but instead of a Savior to contribute to a theology of the Incarnation (without however it constituting a topic for apologetics).

In the biographical material that allows us to form an Image of Christ—*the* God that became man—eschatology predominates.* This predominance means the interpenetration of the two Natures so that any attempt at separation fails. The human and the divine, the day-to-day and the miraculous or the mythic are inseparable, and this inseparability will motivate an astonishing feature of Jung's exegesis. Theologies and theologians will have to decide on their attitude to it. I don't believe there could be any more upsetting vision for them than the one that arose for Jung, exegete of the Incarnation, based on the story of Job. God wanted to make himself man in order to join man—the creature defeated and struck down by him. And then, at a critical moment, from the lips of the God made man, there rises up this desperate cry, "My God, my God, why have you forsaken me?" As if having no respite right up to the extreme moment, God become man had to experience himself, in his own turn, the despair formerly inflicted by him on his servant Job.†

For this cry of divine despair to resound in a soul as an "answer

---

*Jung, *Antwort auf Hiob*, 74ff.
†Jung, *Antwort auf Hiob*, 76.

to Job" requires that a very secret depth be attained. Should we be surprised if this soul bounds back from these depths with a power that dares to formulate ultimate questions? Jung places us in front of this dilemma: In the final analysis, can Christ be understood and interpreted *today* by men of today, or instead must we be subjected to the weight of history and content ourselves with the interpretation established by generations of theologians, councils, and synods?* In other terms, there is a traditional concept that nothing less than the sacrifice of the Son of God would be able to appease the "wrath of the Father." What then is this Father who demands that his son be butchered, rather than forgiving these unfortunate creatures delivered by him into the clutches of satanic power? And there would be another concept: A concept that considers the work of reconciliation not as the payment of a human debt toward God, but rather as the reparation of a divine injustice toward the human being.† It is for each individual to experience within himself where the divine grandeur is felt, and if the feeling of it necessarily postulates this complex of guilt that we see reappearing in our times, in a secularized and abject form.

This overturning of the traditional concept has nothing in common with the rationalist objections that have been set forth on numerous occasions in the past about the case of Job. His motivation is related rather to the feeling experienced by so many mystics, so many spiritual individuals, since the time that Christianity first existed. And this is why Jung can give a lesson to the theologians who formerly proposed "de-mythologizing" (*entmythologisieren*) the figure of Christ. It is perhaps the same ignorance or disdain, let us say, that enabled the rationalism of the last century to reduce this figure to a myth, and that has enabled certain theologians of

---

*Compare with Jung, *Antwort auf Hiob,* 94.
†Jung, *Antwort auf Hiob,* 92.

today (even without knowing it) to rationalize it while claiming to "de-mythologize" it. One way or another, it is the same ignorance of the reality of myth. "The myth is not a *fiction*."* The birth and the destiny of a God in time does not get announced in the same way as that of a religious reformer. What is a religion without myth when religion means very precisely the function that puts us in communication with eternal myth?† Myth remains perhaps the figure of a religious master more or less well attested historically—perhaps a Pythagoras or a Muhammad—but in no case a son of God, incarnating Yahweh's project of becoming man. Myth can move and be crystalized into dogma. It is the situation that has been experienced that will ensure the "valorization" of the myth. To those who seek to valorize the myth in the presence of the symbolism of the two natures or in the presence of the life of a God and the life of a man united in the person of Christ, Jung issues the reminder that myth takes place in the human being. He reminds us that human beings are totally possessed by the archetype—they will have mythic destinies just as much as the Greek heroes. "That the life of Christ was to a great extent a myth does not detract in any way from its positive reality. I would say just the opposite! Because the mythic character of a life expresses precisely the universal human validity of that life."‡

However, not everything has been accomplished. A dark threat persists, which we can see being expressed in the sixth request in the prayer "Our Father:" Do not lead us into temptation. (*Et ne nos inducas . . .*) This is too often translated modestly by "Do not let us give in to . . ." Quite regularly, as men have been baptized, it is not from their sins that humanity is delivered but from "fear of the consequences of the sin—that is, God's anger." The work of salvation then is to deliver men

---

*Jung, *Antwort auf Hiob*, 77.

†Jung, *Antwort auf Hiob*, 77.

‡Jung, *Antwort auf Hiob*, 77.

from the fear of God.* So the sixth request translates a fear, like the presentiment of the coming of he who could seduce even the Chosen ones themselves. This servitude to fear must be abolished in order for there truly to be a reign of the religion of love. In this way, we are led toward what constitutes the third act of the drama that unfolds in the book: the Book of Revelation (Apocalypse of John). And we are led there by a development of prophetic Consciousness from the grand vision of Ezekiel in the Books of Enoch, postulating with the divine anthropomorphosis the evangelical promise of the reign of the Holy Spirit.

With the succession of these visions (they span from the sixth to the first centuries BCE) there emerges an archetype that comes to be impressed on human Consciousness more and more urgently. Quite rightly, Jung rejects the pitiful rationalist argument claiming that Ezekiel's visions are of a pathological character. A vision does not *eo ipso* reveal a pathological nature. Without being frequent, the phenomenon is not rare in normal human beings either. It follows a natural process that cannot be qualified as pathological unless, in a given case, a pathological nature is shown to be present.† The two great themes that arise mainly from the visions of Ezekiel and Daniel are those of the Son of Man and of the quaternity—this symbol of archetypical wholeness, the whole "I." Jung's last books have returned to the analysis of this symbol with insistence. In this sense, the Book of Enoch would call for a whole fertile amplification. Actually, it is not only the Book of Enoch that ought to be involved, but we would need to include the books commonly designated as 2 Enoch and 3 Enoch (the figure of Enoch–Metatron–Archangel Michael). We need to mention further how equating Enoch (Idris) to Hermes in Islam, and notably in Islamic gnosis, would allow us to make a concordance with

---

*Jung, *Antwort auf Hiob*, 89.
†Jung, *Antwort auf Hiob*, 96.

the results obtained by Jung with respect to Hermes in alchemy and Hermeticism.

Let us mention here only the meaning that the figure of Enoch presents for the analysis:* Enoch is not simply a receptacle of divine Revelation. He is drawn into and included in the divine drama as if he were at least a son of God. Everything takes place as if what was corresponding to the divine anthropomorphosis were an apotheosis, or at least an angelomorphosis of the human being—that is, his inclusion in the pleromatic Event. Because not only is the Son of Man described as one "who possesses justice," who accompanied the Ancient of days and "whose countenance resembled that of man and was full of grace, like that of one of the holy angels,"† but finally Enoch himself is addressed by the *angelus interpres* with the title of "Son of Man." Enoch recognizes himself thus in the rapture as Son of Man or rather Son of God. He is completely assimilated by the divine mystery he has been witness to and takes his place in Heaven. Already the appellation given to Ezekiel of "Son of Man" suggests that the Incarnation and the divine quaternity were, in the pleroma, the prototype of what was to happen, due to the divine anthropomorphosis, not simply to the Son of God foreseen for all eternity but to the human being as such. Intuitive anticipation is achieved in Enoch, who becomes ecstatically the Son of Man;‡ his being carried away in the chariot (like Elijah) prefigures the resurrection of the dead. It is superfluous to entertain Christian interpolations in order to "explain" visions and doctrines here. However, with respect to the question of knowing if—and to what extent—Christianity actually marks the irruption in history of something absolutely new, doubtless we can only respond to that question by distinguishing an aspect of Christianity (typified for example

---

*Jung, *Antwort auf Hiob,* 102ff.
†Enoch 46:1.
‡Jung, *Antwort auf Hiob,* 107.

by the motif of *Christos-angelos*) that in the end was not the one offi-cially adopted by Christianity in history. This is such a necessary dis-tinction that it becomes the driving force of the drama.

Effectively, what happens to Enoch, in his capacity as an ordi-nary and mortal man, can happen to others besides him. To the pos-sibility of the Event (which was only ecstatic anticipation in Enoch), there corresponds the evangelical promise of the sending forth of the Paraclete, the Holy Spirit by whom the Christ was engendered, and by whom God will be engendered in creatural man.* This incarnation by the Holy Spirit amounts to saying: a continuous and progressive Incarnation. "He who believes in me will do works that I do, and he will do also greater ones."† "I have said, 'You are *gods*. You are sons of the Very-High.'"‡ No ecclesiastical or sociopolitical interpretation can be substituted here. It is in each human individual, as such, that the mystery of salvation is to be accomplished. However, this individua-tion from and through incarnation can only be the work of Sophia.

Because it is precisely here that the antinomy bursts forth, and that the threat of the Antichrist is betrayed. Under Christianity, Satan's reign is not over. The action of the Paraclete, metaphysically so important, is entirely undesirable for the proper organization of a church because that action is beyond any control. Consequently, there will be a strong affirmation of the uniqueness of the fact of the Incarnation, and the progressive taking up of residency in man by the Holy Spirit will be discouraged or ignored. Whoever feels carried by the Holy Spirit toward "deviations" is a "heretic." His rooting out and his extermination are both necessary and conformable to Satan's tastes.§ Certainly, Christianity would have succumbed to a Babel-like

---

*Jung, *Antwort auf Hiob,* 111ff.
†John 14:12.
‡Psalms 82:6.
§Jung, *Antwort auf Hiob,* 114.

confusion if each individual had been able to impose the intuitions of his Holy Spirit and constrain others to those intuitions. But finally it is just in human *individuals* that it is incumbent upon the Holy Spirit to take up residence and act so as to remind them of what Christ taught. Now it is these individuals who either undergo the authoritarian collective constraint, or claim, each one of them, to constrain others. Here there is denounced the painful internal contradiction: the promise of the Holy Spirit and the impossibility of its reign. For this reign can come about only in those precise conditions that the Holy Spirit itself can produce. And in the meantime the accomplished type of human being that perfected *individuation* represents (in Jung's technical sense of this word) will remain an exception or a heroic act.

The annunciation, however, has been given, and it is upon the annunciation that the third act of the drama moves to its climax. This act opens now with the Book of Revelation. This whole last part of the book achieves the transmission of the deepest and most personal of Jung's experiences. His exegesis is so intimately connected to discoveries in his psychology that unless we are able to insist on his psychology and its lexicon, we fear that we will betray his exegesis by being too brief.

3. The Exaltation of Sophia

Three broad leitmotifs follow. There is the terrifying Apparition of a Christ merged with the Ancient of days. From his mouth comes "a double-edged sword."* If John falls down "as dead," it is certainly not *love* but rather *fear* that strikes him down.† There is the no less terrifying Apparition of the Lamb with its "seven horns." The opening of the sixth seal provokes a cosmic catastrophe "before the anger of the Lamb, for the great day of his anger has come."‡ Paradox: the world

---

*Revelation 1:16.

†Jung, *Antwort auf Hiob,* 117ff.

‡Revelation 6:16–17.

that was endeavored to be restored in a state of innocence and love is plunged into fire and blood—no longer a trace of Christian kindness, forgiving of one's enemies, or love. All of that represents the negative side of the Christian Event. But when the seventh angel has sounded his trumpet, there is the Apparition of "the Woman attired with the sun, the moon below her feet and a crown of twelve stars on her head . . . The dragon stays in front of the woman about to give birth so he can devour her child . . . and her child was taken away toward God and toward his throne, and the woman flees toward the desert where she had a place prepared by God."* From the contemplation of this vision there will be projected the high vault where the Assumption of the Virgin will resound as *the* "answer to Job."

As we know, the vision is introduced by the opening of the Temple in Heaven and the Apparition of the *Arca fœderis* (symbol of the Virgin in the *Litaniae*). She is a prelude to the descent of the bride Heavenly Jerusalem, the equivalent of Sophia. She is provided with cosmic attributes that transform her into an *anima mundi* to such an extent that we can see in her the primordial feminine Anthropos (*der weibliche Urmensch*) and the masculine Anthropos. Heaven above; Heaven below. These symbols indicate the mystery of the heavenly Woman: she contains in the darkness of her breast the sun of "masculine" Consciousness that is rising, like a child, from the nocturnal sea of the Unconscious, and that, as an old man, is returning to this transconsciousness. The vision is a part, an anticipation of the *hieros gamos* of which the result is a divine Child.† It announces the hierogamy of opposites, the reconciliation of Nature with Spirit. The divine child, the Filius Sapientiae, that in this heavenly hierogamy engenders Sophia, he too is a *complexion oppositorum,* a unifying symbol, a totality of life.

---

*Revelation 12:1, 12:4–6.
†Jung, *Antwort auf Hiob,* 122–23, 127.

A current exegesis tends to confuse the birth of this Child with the birth of the Christ Child—which happened a long time ago and in quite different circumstances—or, alternatively, to consider the Child as a double of "he who must shepherd nations with an iron rod."* This is really about the *birth* of a divine Child. It is not a *return* of Christ himself because Christ must come "on the clouds of Heaven,"† and not be born or engendered a second time, and even less would he be born from the conjunction of the sun and the moon. In fact, the Child "taken away toward God" does not appear again in the Book of Revelation. This is why Jung tended to see in the whole episode an interpolation in the course of Johannine visions. And nevertheless it is definitely the figure of this Child that dominates the whole last part of the book and the future that he partially reveals.

The figure of the Filius Sapientiae is intimately associated here with the idea of an ongoing Incarnation, and it is through the experience of the John of the Book of Revelation that the connection will filter through (as it already does in the person of Enoch). Because the personage of the ecstatic and of the visionary is essentially included and implied and in the Event.‡ John is taken and gripped by the archetype of the divine son; his unconscious personality identifies closely with Christ. He sees how God is born once again in the Unconscious, without it being discernable to John's Self—the divine Child being the symbol of both one and the other. In this sense, John is anticipating Jakob Böhme and the Alchemists; his personal implication in the divine drama is something he experiences as arriving ahead of this divine birth in man that the Alchemists, Meister Eckhart, and Angelus Silesius foresaw.§ Psychologically it is a question of the rela-

---

*Revelation 2:27.
†Matthew 24:30.
‡Jung, *Antwort auf Hiob*, 125–26, 128.
§Jung, *Antwort auf Hiob*, 139.

tionship between the Self, which transcends Consciousness, and the "I," which is limited to this Consciousness. It's a matter of the superiority of the perfected man (*téleios*)—that is total superiority, being constituted of one and the other. The relationship can be typified in the relationship Christ–man. Out of this some undeniable analogies emerge between certain Indian and Christian concepts.*

However, John's issue is not a personal problem nor is it reducible to a personal situation. We are speaking here of visions that spring forth from more abyssal depths, because John is expressing himself in archetypal forms and what he says must be explained by the archetypal Event. He sees into the far distant future of the Christian aeon. He foresees a monstrous course in the opposite direction, and he understands this future only as the annihilation of the Darkness that has not received the Light. But he does not see that this furor of hate and wrath, this devastation and vengeance very precisely *is* the Darkness from which God become man was separated. What has become of the religion of love? The passion that filters through in his Revelation is infinitely more than a deeply felt personal feeling: "It is the spirit of God himself moving through the fragile human envelope, and, once again, it demands *fear* of men in the face of unfathomable divinity."†

Now our own world has been shaken by too many monstrous trials for the question not to have become a burning question for so many men of today. One way or another, can all of this be reconciled with a "God who is good"? We have arguments that traditionally we have held ready in response. Have they dried a single tear? Are they today an "answer to Job"? Are not Job's good friends and consolers responsible for Job having preferred quite simply to become agnostic? Jung says of this: "Here we no longer have a problem deriving from

---

*Jung, *Antwort auf Hiob,* 127.
†Jung, *Antwort auf Hiob,* 130.

the scholarly specialty of theologians. This is a universally human, religious nightmare. Though I am uninitiated in theology, I can bring a contribution to the treatment of this question; indeed, perhaps even I *must*."* The paradoxical contradiction in the essence of divinity tears man apart too and leads him into apparently unsolvable conflicts. As a psychotherapist, Jung can speak here from his long experience of souls and the healing of souls. But he invites each individual, though they may be lacking this experience, to become knowledgeable about how this divine tearing apart was experienced and then vanquished in the consciousness of men who have left us the extraordinary testimony consisting of alchemical documents.

Here, we cannot even give the summary of a summary. Each individual must move into an analysis based on an extensive documentation. Here the essential reminder bears on the true object of Hermetic philosophy: the *conjunctio oppositorum*. Hermetic philosophy designates its Child in one aspect as a "stone" and in another aspect as homunculus, Filius Sapientiae, Filius Solis et Lunae, *homo altus*. This is exactly the form that we encounter in the Book of Revelation as the son of the Woman clothed with the Sun, and whose birth is like a paraphrase of the birth of the Christ Child. As we know, Jung's great and surprising discovery was realizing that this motif astonishingly reappears in the dreams of men who know nothing at all about alchemy—"as if the Alchemists had foreseen what kind of problem would be posed in the future by the Book of Revelation." The question that preoccupied the Alchemists for close to seventeen hundred years is the same question that oppresses modern man.†

The conflict introduced by Christianity is this: God wished and wants to become man. And John experienced in his vision a second

*Jung, *Antwort auf Hiob*, 144.
†Jung, *Antwort auf Hiob*, 146.

birth of the Son, having Sophia as his mother. This birth is characterized by the *conjunctio oppositorum;* it is a divine birth that anticipates the Filius Sapientiae, and it is the very substance of the process of
individuation.* This Son is the *mediator* of opposites. The conclusion
that traditional Christian theology came to was *omne bonum a Deo,
omne malum ab homine.* This conclusion maintains the old Yahweh
heritage of the opposition between God and man. As such, it gives
to man a cosmic and overdrawn grandeur in evil. It charges him with
carrying the whole *dark* side of divinity. The irruption of apocalyptic
visions is enough to give some idea of what then takes place.† However,
this irruption produces in John the Image of the divine Child, the
Savior to come, born of the divine companion whose Image lives in
every man, the Child that Meister Eckhart (he too) contemplated in a
vision. Because the shadow side in God is something for God himself
to abolish, and this is done precisely by his becoming man and by his
being born of Sophia. The Incarnation of Christ is then the prototype
that is progressively transferred to the creature by the Holy Spirit, the
promised Paraclete. The Filius Sapientiae is thus he through whom
the Holy Spirit accomplishes the divine anthropomorphosis—a God
of love in a man of gentleness. He is engendered from an "unknown
father" and from Sophia-Sapientia. Certainly, for that, "Christian virtues" are needed, but they are not enough. This is not only a moral
issue. Wisdom is needed—the wisdom Job was looking for and up
until his anamnesis remained hidden to Yahweh. This *filius* represents
the totality that transcends consciousness in the form or figure of Puer
aeternus. It is in the Child that Faust is resuscitated transformed. It
is to him that the following evangelical statement refers: "Unless you
become like children . . ."‡—that is, a child born of the maturity of

---

*Jung, *Antwort auf Hiob,* 147.
†Jung, *Antwort auf Hiob,* 148.
‡Matthew 18:3.

the age of man and not the unconscious child that many would like to remain or become.* All the symbols brought to light in Jung's books and extensive research crowd in together here, adding their voices severally as a final chorus of a new "second Faust."

It is there in fact, in the only Faustian choir of the invisible church that the Assumption of the *Mater Gloriosa* can today be celebrated as the annunciation of the heavenly hierogamy from which there will proceed the Filius Sapientiae—he who will conduct the healing and will lead the human being, until now fragmented, into his wholeness. For mankind, this is what the approach of the Virgin Mother has always meant. The Woman robed in sun belongs to another world, a world to come. It is in Heaven that the final chapter of the Apocalypse or Revelation comes to a close, and it is through a *hiero gamos* as in every process of individuation. Here there unfolds what is properly Jung's prophetic and eschatological perspective. The conjunction of the Light with the Light, the divine Incarnation within creatural man, presupposes the completion and the end of the Christian aeon. The vision of the heavenly Woman means the dawning of a new aeon.

What we see becoming more precise here is the interdependence and correlation of two Events: the final Sophianic hierogamy of the Apocalypse and the Assumption of the Virgin—the Exaltation of Maria-Sophia. This correlation is the heralding and the guarantee of the divine Incarnation, not in the sense of a repetition of the birth of God, but in the sense of an Incarnation continuing in creatural man, and begun with Christ.† Because the nuptial union in the heavenly *thalamos,* the *hieros gamos,* is the first degree of the birth of the Savior, who since Antiquity has been hailed as Filius Solis et Lunae, Filius Sapientiae, and corresponding to Christ.‡ It is this expectation

---

*Jung, *Antwort auf Hiob,* 150–51.
†Compare with Jung, *Antwort auf Hiob,* 158.
‡Compare with Jung, *Antwort auf Hiob,* 157.

that popular Catholic nostalgia interprets still today—a nostalgia that, by calling on wishes for the Exaltation of the Mother of God manifests its aspiration to the *mediator pacem faciens inter inimicos.*[*]

No doubt birth is eternal and forever in the pleroma. But birth in time can only happen if it is perceived, recognized, and declared by man.[†] And it is right here that we see the historicity of the Event in its eminent reality as a psychic Event, which is a true rapport between Time and Eternity. Historical science, regardless of what it might expect, cannot perceive this so long as it remains a "natural history." And this is why, in Jung's judgment, the year 1950 marks the date of the most important religious Event since the Reformation. The birth of the Filius Sapientiae, the continued divine incarnation in creatural man, means that in the consciousness of creatural man the deity has totally abolished its shadow side and its furor. The Darkness has finally received the Light and the Light has taken and captured the shadow and the furor. No more divine wrath toward man and correlatively no more human terror exploding in furor. In shedding his shadow side, God unburdens man of it. God is born to man and man is born to God as Filius Sapientiae, son of Sophia. This is no longer only the anamnesis of Sophia, as in the Old Testament, but her reign and her exaltation, because we have here her mediatory work. She is the defender and the witness, the advocate in Heaven, and *that* is the answer to Job.

No doubt all of that is rather far from the real intentions that motivated the pontifical definition of the new dogma. However, the objection would not come up against the proposal established here any more than does the weight of historical criticism produced against the dogma of the Assumption from the side of its opponents (Protestant

---

[*]Jung, *Antwort auf Hiob,* 157.
[†]Jung, *Antwort auf Hiob,* 157.

or Catholic). The latter have even something ridiculous about them since the action of the Holy Spirit in the private recesses of the soul and of souls necessarily goes beyond rationalist historicism. It is also somewhat paradoxical to see the psychologist Jung highlight the method of pontifical "demonstration," which is outrageous to rational understanding to the extent that it bases its support on prefigurations that can be neither despised nor omitted and on a more than millennial tradition. The material of proof in favor of the psychic phenomenon is more than sufficient. Shall we say that the arguments tend to support a physically impossible phenomenon? Very well, "all religious affirmations are *physical* impossibilities."*

There is another objection that has come to light against the new dogma, especially on the side of the Protestants. It is the fear that the since Mother of God (Deipara, Theotokos) is infinitely close to the deity, Christ's supremacy might be shaken. But are we then to forget how every Protestant hymnal is full of references to the "heavenly bridegroom"? Shouldn't this bridegroom have a bride with equality under the law? Or is all that nothing but a metaphor? Would we prefer to confess that we are only able to represent and accept a "religion of males" (Männerreligion), of men incapable of conceiving of a metaphysical representation of a Woman? However, the bride cannot be replaced by the Church any more than Christ can be replaced by an organization. "The Feminine no less than the Masculine demands to be represented in a person."†—I believe that we ought to mention again, as a support, the whole Sophianic tradition of Lutheran men of the spirit (Jakob Böhme, V. Weigel, G. Arnold, G. Gichtel, Œtinger, and so on).

Out of all the thoughts that have been condensed here in the

---

*Jung, *Antwort auf Hiob,* 160.
†Jung, *Antwort auf Hiob,* 161.

extreme, there emerges the sense that there could have been for Jung a certain question that he was often asked. It is the same question that Gretchen asked of Faust: *"Glaubst du an Gott?"* (Do you believe in God?)* Let us not return to the reproach of "psychologizing." The truth is that Jung committed the originality, while working on psychology, of holding that the *psyche* is real, whereas so many others would only accept psychic facts as real. ("This amounts," he said, "to thinking that uranium and laboratory apparatuses are all you need to make the bomb.") He does not imagine that the psychic Event is dissolved in an illusory smoke because it has been "explained." And we must hold firmly to that. God is a psychic reality. We can be aware of him only psychically, not physically. There are no "proofs" that weigh for or against his existence. Regarding what we will consider in the following pages, a certain familiarity with Jung's work is required in order to avoid misunderstanding his Hermeneutic and his valorization of symbols. I am making a point of saying this in order to avoid any misunderstanding.†

Already the ongoing divine Incarnation in creatural man, through the mediation of Sophia, indicates here the only direction from which it is possible for there to come experimentally a response to the question, "Glaubst du an Gott?" I can recognize "as real only that which acts on me; what is not acting on me might very well not exist."‡ Now,

---

*See Jung, *Antwort auf Hiob,* 159ff.
†Compare notably *Paracelsus as a Spiritual Phenomenon,* in *Alchemical Studies,* translated by R. F. C. Hull, vol. 13 of the *Collected Works of C. G. Jung* (Princeton, N.J.: Princeton University Press, 1968); *Psychology and Alchemy,* translated by R. F. C. Hull, vol. 12 of the *Collected Works of C. G. Jung* (Princeton, N.J.: Princeton University Press, 1980); *Die Psychologie der Übertragung, Erläutert anhand einer alchemistischen Bilderserie* [The psychology of transmission, explained using an alchemical series of pictures] (Zürich: Rascher Verlag, 1946); *Symbolik des Geistes: Studien über psychische Phänomenologie* [Symbolism of the mind: studies on psychic phenomenology] (Zürich: Rascher Verlag, 1948).
‡Jung, *Antwort auf Hiob,* 167.

if the deity is acting on us, we can be aware of it only by means of the psyche. However, just at this point, is there a possibility of discerning whether the action comes from God or from the depths of the Unconscious and also can we determine that what we have here is two different greatnesses? Even if the question goes beyond analytical psychology as such, it doesn't mean it can't be asked of psychology. Now, the response, which here has the advantage of being completely experimental, is revealed to the extent in which the coming birth of the divine Child in creatural man—result of the heavenly hierogamy in the pleroma to which the Assumption of the Virgin Mother refers—is recognized as a metaphysical Event or process constituting a process of *individuation* par excellence.*

We have here a central and fundamental notion in Jung's psychology and therapy. It is possible to perceive a certain resonance with Schleiermacher and Leibniz.† The flowering of this process in the fullness of Consciousness requires a confrontation between Consciousness and the Unconscious and the achievement of a balance between these two opposites. However, in terms of *logic,* this process is neither possible nor expressible; only *symbols* make possible the irrational fusion of opposites. These symbols emerge spontaneously from the Unconscious; the Consciousness develops them further. What brings to light and points to the central symbols of the process of individuation is the Self, or in other words, the totality of the human being who is made up of, on the one hand, what he is conscious of, and on

---

*Jung, *Antwort auf Hiob,* 165.

†It is not by chance that Leibniz occupies such an important place among the "precursors of the idea of synchronicity" in the Jung's study on the subject, *Synchronizität als ein Prinzip akausaler Zusammenhänge* [*Synchronicity: An Acausal Connecting Principle*], vol. 4, *Studien aus dem C. G. Jung-Institut Zürich,* edited by C. A. Meier (Zürich: 1952), 83ff. On the notions of the individual and individuation, see *Types psychologiques,* préface et traduction Y. Le Lay, Genève, 1950, index s.v. and p. 470 *et seq.*

the other hand, the contents of the nonconscious that transcends the Conscious. The Self is a *téleios anthropos,* the "perfected man" (well known by all mystic gnostics) whose symbols are the divine Child, Filius Sapientiae, Filius Solis et Lunae.* *Habet mille nomina,* as the Alchemists said, meaning that, from the causal point of view, the principle and the outcome of the process of individuation (Self regeneration) are an *ineffabile.*† Strictly speaking, the Image of God does not coincide with the Unconscious pure and simple, "but rather with one particular element of its contents—namely, the archetype of the Self. It is from this archetype that we can empirically separate the Image of God."‡ It is scarcely necessary to emphasize the import of these analyses for present-day research in religious phenomenology.

What we are saying here is perhaps both too much and too little to provoke a fertile contemplation and avoid any misunderstanding. I would like however to add this: he who has attained this individuation and has become conscious of the rich depths that are strictly his own and not transmissible, and in which there resides his image and his idea of divinity—such a man will finally realize the truth of those simple words so often emitted with a pathetic flippancy: *my* God. And in this rigorous and privileged individuation of the relationship between the human being and *his* divinity, we can perceive something of an echo of a striking thought of Luther's that puts realization in correspondence with faith: "The God I will have will be the one in whom I believe."§ Finally, let us not imagine that the idea of the divine Incarnation in empirical man through the *inhabitatio* of the Holy Spirit would justify some *hybris* or other with an Anabaptist flavor. Jung knows it and reminds us, as a conclusion, about the ethical

---

*Compare with Jung, *Antwort auf Hiob,* 165.
†Compare with Jung, *Antwort auf Hiob,* 166.
‡Jung, *Antwort auf Hiob,* 167.
§I am quoting from memory.

consequences of "the splinter in the flesh."* Man, even when enlightened, remains what he is "and is never more than his limited "I" in the face of he who lives within him and whose form has no knowable limits, the one who envelops him on all sides, deep as abysmal reaches of the Earth, immense as the spaces of Heaven."†

III

I hope that the summaries and paraphrases will have been faithful enough to Jung's thought to allow the intentions and motifs of *Answer to Job* to be understood. It is still too soon to judge the agreement and the contradiction that this book has already encountered and will continue to encounter. Perhaps one day the author will appear as a prophet of eternal Sophia. I confess that I have reread the book somewhat in the fashion of an oratorio that might one day occur to a future Handel: its score would be made up solely of sacred texts, but drawn from not just canonical books but from deuterocanonical books and from the so-called apocryphal books as well. It would end with a soothing choir of alto voices, proclaiming the hymn attributed to Albertus Magnus and which formerly found its place in the *Missa alchemica* of Melchior Cibinensis: *Ave praeclara maris stella . . .*‡

But it is not at all with projects of musical composition that we embarked on commenting here on *Answer to Job*. I referred at the beginning to Kierkegaard, Father Bulgakov, and the science of religions in general. These three topics researched on a comparative basis would require a whole book. We are only making brief sketches of them here.

---

*2 Corinthians 12:7.
†Jung, *Antwort auf Hiob*, 169.
‡Compare with *Psychologie und Alchemie*, 538ff.

1. Kierkegaard, the "Christian Job"

If Kierkegaard discovered his own archetype in the destiny of Job, it would have been on the occasion of the painful episode of his engagement to Regine Olsen, an episode that is very far from announcing something resembling Sophianic feeling. In short, it is not a question for him of bringing an "answer to Job," but actually of imitating him, of reproducing an exemplary case—that is to say, the case of repetition in which the hero is placed back into the original situation. But being placed back in the original situation is to be placed into memory—it is intentionally *losing* what is present, what is presented, and finding oneself in a state of the purely possible while appropriating that as a memory. And doing that because here memory is not a recalling of the past but an entry of eternity into time. I think there is a lot to learn through the contrast between the idea of repetition and the process of individuation referred to earlier. Kierkegaard dared come to the lucid realization: "Christianity exists because there is hatred between God and men." But can the way to the lost paradise of love be found again if the passageway from the perceptible to the spiritual has been definitively destroyed, if Jacob's ladder has been forever broken? Here there must be a reversal of a philosophic order according to which the act arises from the potential possible. The lost paradise is no longer a potential. The possible from the impossible will be born (and reborn) from the act, from the ordeal of initiatory faith that allows the divine Incarnation to individualize itself in the creatural human being and to announce itself to him by having him reborn as Filius Sapientiae. "If I had had faith," said Kierkegaard, "I would still be with Regine."

2. Sophiology

In contrast, it is a symphonic relationship that we can perceive between the Sophiology of Father Bulgakov and what can also be called the Sophiology of Jung. Certainly, differentials are not absent, and they are the source of some dissonance. The foundation itself differs based on the fact that the thought of the Russian Orthodox theologian moves within the framework of traditional Christian dogmatism, whereas Jung's thought proceeds with complete, nondenominational freedom. The Sophiology itself represents an interpretation of the world, a theological weltanschauung within Christianity. It was a direction of theological thought at the heart of the Orthodox Church. It did not constitute a dominant thread as did Thomism or Modernism in the Catholic Church of the West.* It is represented nevertheless by a long tradition, from Solovyov to Father Florensky. Because of the way in which it poses the relationship between God and the world, between God and man, and because of its affinity with the thought of Meister Eckhart, Böhme, Schelling, and Baader, it is doubtless today, among all the currents of Christian theology, the school that is best able to understand Jung's Sophianic message.

Its point of departure can be thought of as a confrontation between the Aristotelian concept of substance (*ousia*)—a concept used by the Greek Fathers in their thinking about immanent hypostatic relationships of the divine Trinity—and the figures, given in the Bible (especially in the wisdom books), of Sophia (Wisdom) and Doxa (Glory) (Shekhina). These figures cannot be, as the exegesis sometimes maintains, simple divine attributes, properties, or qualities. Furthermore, if the divine essence varies in them, the ousia is nothing but an abstract and empty metaphysical schema. The whole effort was brought to bear to show that the divinity in God constitutes divine Sophia (or Doxa) and to show that Sophia is the divine ousia, the *locus Triadis*. She is not therefore a hypostasis herself, but she has the power to create of herself a given hypostasis

---

*Compare with Sergius Bulgakov, *The Wisdom of God: A Brief Summary of Sophiology* (London: Paisley Press, 1937), 29.

and to constitute its life.* That is why, strictly speaking, there is no quaternity (the symbol that attracted Jung's attention so strongly). Nevertheless, it was the "danger" of a divine tetrad being substituted for the Triad that led to the hasty judgment of "heresy."

The revelation of the Trinity, as a revelation of the Father who manifests in the hypostases of Logos and of Spirit, is what constitutes the divine life, the divine world, or the eternal Sophia. The mystery of the eternal Sophia as divine ousia is therefore the revelation of the "Father" in the dyad of Logos and Holy Spirit and, as such, this dyad constitutes divine humanity, the heavenly Theantropia. The relationship, which we can consider as being between two principles in the deity, is a relationship that in creatural human beings is reflected in the masculine human being and in the feminine human being.† The world, our cosmos, is produced in the Image of this eternal, divine Sophia. Through her sophianity, the world became the mirror of the divine world, or the *creatural* Sophia. To rise above this redoubling, this duality of the forms of the divine Sophia (the eternal form and the created form) is to make the created into the divine, it is to communicate divine life to it, and to lead it back once again from creatural Sophia to the eternal Sophia. This is what constitutes the theanthropic process.

As briefly as we must speak about it here, this process allows us to glimpse how Sophiology is led to establish between the two events of the Incarnation and the Pentecost, between the epiphany of the Logos and the manifestation of Spirit, an archetypical connection thanks to which the relationships among the figures of the Holy Spirit, Sophia, and the Virgin Mother will be cast in a new light. Quite rightly, Father Bulgakov appeals to the liturgical consciousness

---

*The Wisdom of God, 45ff, 55ff.

†The Wisdom of God, 119–20; compare S. Boulgakov, Le Paraclet: La sagesse divine et la théantropie (Paris: Aubier, 1946), 339ff.

of the Church as being superior to the dogmatic consciousness (and this is an important point for psychology). The liturgical consciousness and the iconographic tradition of the Orthodox Church attest to equating Sophia and the Virgin Mother of God. Christ born of the Virgin is not simply an event isolated in time. It establishes an eternal link between Mother and Son, so that an icon representing the Virgin with her divine Child is, in fact, an Image of divine humanity.* The Virgin in a personal form is the human resemblance of the Holy Spirit. Through her, with her form having become entirely transparent to the Holy Spirit, we have a manifestation, a revelation of the Holy Spirit in the form of a *person*. Divine humanity must in effect be found "on earth as in Heaven" in a *dual* form, not in a single form. The revelation of the Father through Logos and Spirit (inseparably but without confusion), the heavenly Theanthropia, is typified in the Incarnation where "the Son is conceived by the Holy Spirit and born of the Virgin Mary."† The Virgin Mother is the feminine counterpart of the humanity of Christ, and this is why the icon of the Mother of God with her Child (Sophia and Filius Sapientiae!) expresses this Incarnation, this divine humanity.

I have the impression that this metaphysical representation of the Feminine in a person is in harmony with Jung's previously mentioned remarks. With the Sophiologists, there is no longer any abstract speculation at all. Father Bulgakov was an admirable exegete of Russian Orthodox iconography, which attests to the sophianic aspect of the worship of the Mother of God.‡ The sanctuaries of Saint Sophia in

---

The Wisdom of God, 176.

†*The Wisdom of God,* 184.

‡*The Wisdom of God,* 186. The icon of Novgorod presents Wisdom as a fiery angel, with the Virgin on his right and St. John the Baptist on his left. A number of very interesting reproductions of icons of Sophia are to be found in the book by Father Alexis van der Mensbrugghe, *From Dyad to Triad: A Plea for Duality against Dualism and an Essay towards the Synthesis of Orthodoxy* (London: Faith Press, 1935).

the Byzantine Empire bore Christological meaning, and referenced
in Russia a Marian Sophia.* The liturgy finally, connecting a service
specifically about Sophia with that of the Assumption, would suc-
ceed in putting us here in harmony with what we have called the
third act of *Answer to Job*. Its specificity is to bring together the two
interpretations—Byzantine and Russian, of identifying Sophia both
with Christ and with the Virgin Mother of God. Here we have then
the *created* Sophia. "In her, there is achieved the aim of creation,
the complete penetration of the Creation by Wisdom, the complete agreement of the type created with its archetype, its complete
accomplishment."†

3. The Rock of Rhages

The Sophianic idea, the Sophiological principle, acting as a guiding
concept, could have therefore been able to reveal itself as being fertile and useful for the understanding or the hermeneutics of religious
phenomena that very little attention has been paid to up until now,
and for very good reason in the recurrence of the archetype of Sophia.
These pages are being written from the land of Iran, from the high
plateau of Tehran where, on the southern horizon, the rocky crest of
Rhages stands out. Rising up to the level of a symbol, the Rock of
Rhages signals the area of an essential sacred geography. Mentioned in
the Avesta under the name of Ragha, the city was the seat of a small,
Zoroastrian sacerdotal state. And it was to Rhages that there "came"
the archangel Raphael as a messenger to the young Tobias. In Persian
the city is called Rey today and its territory includes a holy Shi'ite
area. We can see outlined among these three motifs topics most dear
to secular Iranian thought and also to the unfolding of Iran's tragedy.

---

*The Wisdom of God, 185.
†The Wisdom of God, 188.

The problem that *Answer to Job* had to confront was that of the integration of the shadow side, the dark aspect of the deity. This becomes a problem waiting to be addressed as soon as the ingeniousness of the speculative intellect gives up dodging the question by substituting for its data a system of metaphysical abstractions. For Jung, as we know, the flight in the face of this questioning that undermines the idea of *Summum Bonum* posed *a priori* results in a concept of Evil that makes this flight into a privation or a lack in being—that is to say, such a concept of Evil abolishes the reality of the flight. However, all the arguments in favor of this concept of Evil as *privatio boni* amount to begging the question (*peticio principii*); everything takes place as if it were already decided that Evil is not and never could be anterior to the existence of man.* There is fear of Manichaeism but the fundamental thought has been being altered for centuries (by confusing the idea of the Counter-Power of Darkness with the idea of a "second God"). The same alteration was continuously committed with respect to Iranian Mazdeism. Jung's thought emerges in utter freedom from a barrage of arguments heaped up by centuries of theology and apologetics that aim to reduce the *positivity* of Evil to a *privatio boni*. It is no small thing that Jung nevertheless addresses the problem with a lucidity that would presuppose a Mazdean cosmology.

With finesse, Charles Andler declared formerly that Nietzsche had been "a Zurvanite without knowing it." There is also indeed in *Answer to Job*† a precise allusion to the Iranian myth of Zurvan, eternal Time "in person," engendering by his thought a Son of Light, Ohrmazd, and by his doubt a Son of Darkness,

---

*Compare notably C. G. Jung, *Aion: Untersuchungen zur Symbolgeschichte* (Zürich: Rascher Verlag, 1951), 76ff.

†Jung, *Antwort auf Hiob,* 27.

Ahriman.* To a certain extent, it would be true to say that the divine drama of *Answer to Job* plays out against a Zurvanite background. It is nonetheless true that Zurvanism could only be in horror of a rigorously Zoroastrian Mazdeism that imposes an uncompromising choice between the Prince of Darkness and the Antagonist. However, as Zoroastrian Mazdeism is, by the very fact, also radically unfamiliar with the subtle metaphysical distinction that authorizes the concept of *privatio boni,* perhaps its world schema could offer neglected resources that would help in thinking about a problem that our epoch posits with painful acuity.

I don't think that we can seriously entertain for an instant the argument sometimes put forward to the effect that materialization of Evil ends up subordinating to itself the good, in the sense that the creature would not then have any other *raison d'être* except that of confronting the Antagonist. First of all, we ought to wonder if the concept of materialization really has any place when it is a question of interpreting a mythic thought. Beside that, the Creation of Light thought by Ohrmazd does not have Ahriman as a *raison d'être*. The combat against Ahriman is not the raison d'être of the terrestrial creature. It is the condition of his existence in the material world that, in the present cosmic period, has become the prey of the Counter-Power of Ahriman. This combat is not the *raison d'être* of the Fravartis or heavenly archetypes; it is the reason for their current terrestrial incarnation. The material world is not in itself a world of Darkness. It is

---

*I have treated the Zurvanite schema and its variations in a study on "Le temps cyclique dans le Mazdéisme et dans l'Ismaélisme" in *Eranos-Jahrbuch* 20 (Zürich: Rhein-Verlag, 1952), 149–217. It is to be noted that Zurvan does not assume the traits of Yahweh. As soon as there appears before him the Son of Light, he becomes aware of his Son of Darkness, and, constrained by his earlier vow, he accords him a reign of only limited duration. In later schemas we see the angel Zurvan triumph over his Darkness and cast it far from himself with the help of other angels (this is a "heavenly combat" that is not exactly that of Revelation 12).

the place of combat, but its being is not subordinate to the combat. The Shadow (the Darkness) is neither identified with man nor transposed on Ohrmazd. Of course, the God of Light, his beauty, his goodness, his gentleness is not the All-Powerful, and the whole theodicy, which cannot bypass the concept of the All-Powerful, lacks precisely the problem and the situation that Zoroastrian Mazdeism has to face.

Much more than the rapport between Creator and creature, Ohrmazd's rapport with the beings of light that proceed from his thought is, since the attack and invasion of the Counter-Power of Ahriman, a rapport between companions in the combat. He needs their help. The Fravartis (*farvahar, ferouër*), celestial archetypes and "tutelary angels" of all celestial and terrestrial creatures, have voluntarily descended for this task in the darkened world. It is not fear that inspires Ohrmazd but rather chivalrous devotion. The suffering that strikes the human being is neither an ordeal nor a punishment that God inflicts on man, who is his companion, his "member." The suffering is evidence of their common enemy. And the suffering of man is the very suffering that the God of Light endures in his "members," from the blows of their enemy. Together they must vanquish him. Because Ahriman is neither an aspect of Ohrmazd, nor a *privatio boni,* there can be no question of integrating him into Creation. He is Counter-Creation, and His presence very precisely means disintegration. The dyadic structure of the being brings together beings of Light, not Light and Darkness.

It is this dyadic structure that is announced in the idea of the Fravarti and it is precisely this same structure that the Rock of Rhages is reminding us of. The archangel Raphael, in his rapport with the young Tobias, corresponds perfectly with the Iranian idea of the Fravarti and with the role that that idea assumes. This identification projects on the little spiritual story of Tobias a perspective that we are not used to considering it from. Other figures of Mazdean angelology filter through the angelology of the Fravarti, especially the figure of Daena, who actually appears as the Mazdean Sophia. And it is through her that all the feminine figures of the angelology and the sacred history of Mazdeism take their meaning, right up to the eschatological figure of the Virgin who will be the Mother of the Savior to come, the Saoshyant who springs forth from the race of Zarathustra—she who is called Omnivictrix or Omniliberatrix (Vispa-taurvairî).

And it was through thinking of this long history of figures that I came to mention earlier a tragedy in Iranian thought and consciousness. Persia became Muslim in the course of the first centuries following the collapse of the national Sassanian power (seventh century). Let us consider the hypothesis of a Sophianic consciousness that suddenly is turned upside down and falls prey to the Yahweh of Job. This tragedy has perhaps not yet ever been properly formulated to our consciousness. And yet, there may well have been also something like an Iranian voice that could give an "answer to Job." This response is graven in the devotion that developed in the form of Shi'ite Islam. Not only do the Holy Imams form a chain of helpful intermediate beings, but especially Fatimah, daughter of the Prophet and Mother of the Holy Imams assumes a role, just as much in the popular piety as in the theosophical speculations of Shi'ism, and especially in Ismaeli Shi'ism, a role that makes of her person a recurrence of the personage of Sophia.

The hypothesis has been formulated recently that the Zoroastrian dualist reform would reveal spiritual connections with pre-Aryan matriarchal civilizations. Let us leave aside any debate about historical causality—for or against. It is of secondary importance. It is much more essential to follow indications that suggest associating with the analysis of Sophianic consciousness the analysis of aspects that have been able to express something of that consciousness in social structures and in the behavior of men. We have no equivalent

in French [or in English —*Trans.*] for *homo, anthropos, Mensch*—
words that designate both the masculine human being and the
feminine human being. It is the concept of their connection that
is in question. Would not the feminine find its "state of metaphysical perfection" only in the masculine, as the virile and patriarchal
civilizations would have it? Or is it rather a question of a dual totality but of which the inherent energy, the vital coherence, and the
perenniality would be thought of as having their source in the feminine? This representation evokes a world that has disappeared and
about which Bachofen, in the past century, had his brilliant intuition. In a recent article this intuition inspired in Raymond Ruyer,
with beautiful ardor, a number of pertinent considerations useful to
our times.*

However, we are speaking of a world that has really disappeared.
The reign of the Holy Spirit Sophia is an eschatological horizon. If it
is true that the Gods who have made themselves men and who suffer
were born first of all in the heart of matriarchal religions, the feminine priesthood of pre-Hellenic peoples and the mystery religions no
longer exist. We no longer have either Theano or Diotima of Mantinea
and the spiritual power invested by them has never had an equivalent
in what is called by this name at the heart of patriarchal masculine
civilizations. What is called "feminism" in our modern societies only
makes us recognize the preponderance and primacy of masculine values, even to the extent of caricaturizing them. Just the opposite of all
that, what would be needed is a world where socialization and special-
ization would no longer rip away from each soul its individuality, its
spontaneous perception of the life of things, and the religious sense
of the beauty of beings. It would be a world where love would have

---

*See Raymond Ruyer, "Pouvoir spirituel et matriarcat," in the *Revue philosophique*
(October–December 1949): 404ff. We must refer equally to the important book by
Erich Neumann, *Ursprungsgeschichte des Bewusstseins* (Zürich: Rascher Verlag, 1949).

to precede all Knowledge, a world where the sense of death would be only nostalgia for resurrection. If all of that even can still be sensed, the conclusion of the second Faust announces it all to us like a mystery of salvation being accomplished by the Eternally Feminine (das Ewig-Weibliche)—as if the call could really come in no other way but one that is met with confident agreement—the urgent call: Die and become.

2

POSTSCRIPT TO
ANSWER TO JOB

Twelve years ago, when the book *Antwort auf Hiob* (1952) appeared, it created a certain stir in German-speaking countries. It passed unnoticed, so to speak, in France, with the exception, so far as we know, of the long article devoted to it by the signator of these lines. That is why Dr. Roland Cahen kindly asked me to take on a complete translation of the book. Alas! Other scholarly and professional obligations prevented me not only from responding to this invitation, but even of assuming any responsibility whatever in the especially difficult task of translating this book.

It will be remembered that, as much from the Protestant side as from the Catholic side, the book was greeted by sometimes vehement criticism. Without a doubt this book falls outside the perspective of traditional Christianity and outside the Christianity of the churches in general. The book is understandable only if we connect its intuitions, which are sometimes stunning and most often unsettling for the ordinary habits of religious thought, to the ensemble of Jung's religious and theological concepts. In doing that, the body of work of the psychologist will then allow us to discover his concepts, reading between the lines if necessary, and the personal memories recorded in his autobiography will then allow us to approach these concepts more closely.

We will close down the meaning of the book if we approach it as a work of biblical criticism. There wasn't even any need for Jung to defend himself as being a professional exegete. There is no question here of a technical exegesis of texts but rather of another exegesis: the exegesis of a soul and of souls, and of their most personal, innermost secret. And after all, is there even one single scholarly exegesis where there is not present, even if tacitly but quite definitely, the exegesis of the soul of the exegete? But here the postulate is frankly confessed, and we see the force of the man in his intimate encounter with the Bible— an attitude that could proceed only from a specifically Protestant spiritual origin.

Penetrated as I was by this conviction, I endeavored to give the book a rather long analysis, amplified by a more personal interpretation and commentary. Already, in the course of the preceding years, I had had occasion to meet Jung several times in our summer sessions of the Eranos circle at Ascona in Switzerland. The article, which I immediately sent to him, inspired him to write a letter, the text of which, through certain personal precisions that he brought, seemed to us—to Dr. Roland Cahen and myself—that it needed to be inserted as a postscript to the present translation. In fact, not only does Jung give his complete approval to the way in which I have oriented and orchestrated the phases of his *Answer to Job,* but also he notes how the inspiration for the book came to him. He confesses having a moment of joy contrasting with melancholy that he experienced in facing a vigilant lack of understanding. And, above all, he claims a spiritual ascendance that is perhaps not admitted to so explicitly in his books. It must be believed then that we have here a document that cannot detract from efforts that will tend, in the future, to deepen the meaning of Jung's thought and his body of work.

The article in question was not written by a professional psychologist; that I am not. But the encounter of the researcher in religious sciences with Jung's psychology operates from the very fact that this psychology dares to speak the word *soul* and to put "man on the way to discovering his soul." Also, this psychology can guide a religious phenomenology that accepts as a postulate the *reality* of its object—with all that that implies. This phenomenology is differentiated from the phenomenology of historical consciousness, in force since Hegel, by the fact that it always begins with the *prehistory* of the soul because this prehistory is not shut away in the past, not closed and left behind with the past, but always imminent, always there, "at the beginning." This is why his schema differs from the classical plan of the "history of salvation," as it is maintained in all traditional Christian dogmatics.

What Jung treated in his book is, in a way, a phenomenology of religion or of Sophianic consciousness. The connections behind that treatment find their roots in the ensemble of his research scrutinizing the symbols and the secret of alchemy as a mystery of deliverance for the soul. That deliverance comes about through the soul's birthing of itself, its individuation. The culminating figure in this mystery is that of the Virgo Sophia, as *anima caelestis* of the adept. Thus, the task of the phenomenology is to analyze the conditions that place the soul in the presence of that figure— that is, to analyze what happens in the soul, *when* it happens, and *so that* it happens that the figure of Sophia appears on the soul's horizon.

The latent drama in *Answer to Job* is articulated in the order of the books of the Bible—both the canonical and the so-called apocryphal—introduced and commented on by Jung. First of all, the Book of Job, then the wisdom books, and finally the Book of Enoch leading to the visions of the Johannine Apocalypse in the Book of Revelation. In outlining his intentions, in such a way as to accentuate the modulation and assuring each time a smooth transition from one to the next, I adapted the work into a schema of three major acts, with given themes respectively as follows: (1) The Absence of Sophia: this is the Book of Job with Yahweh's outbursts of wrath. The curtain falls on Job's silence. (2) The anamnesis or the "rememorization" of Sophia. Emerging from this silence, we have the idea of Sophia or Divine Wisdom (Sapientia Dei), the Spirit (Pneuma) of feminine nature, invested with the reality of a hypostasis, with the reality of a person, and preexisting before Creation. As the reader will see, Jung has collected and amplified here the most beautiful Biblical texts, which constitute something like the Old Testament of the "Sophianic religion." The voice of Sophia, "forgotten" by Yahweh for the whole length of the Book of Job, resonates like that of the "Advocate or Witness in Heaven" invoked by Job. (3) Then we have the Exaltation of Sophia, the third act in which the leitmotifs culminate in the vision of the Apocalypse, the Apparition of the "Woman robed with the sun," prelude to the descent of the celestial bride, Jerusalem. She is the figure of the primordial feminine Anthropos (der weibliche Urmensch), the mystery of the heavenly Woman, containing in the darkness of her breast the sun of "masculine" consciousness that rises up, like a child, from the nocturnal sea of the Unconscious, in order to return, as an old man, to the transconsciousness in which there operates the redemption of Faust, *renovatus in novam infantiam*. This is because the child that the evangelical words are referring to is not the unconscious child that many individuals would like to remain, but the child who is born of the maturity of the age of man.

The vision offers then something like an anticipation of the *heiros gamos,* of the hierogamy whose result is the divine Child. God is born to man and man is born to God as Filius Sapientiae, the son of Sophia. The Incarnation of Christ is then the prototype that is transferred progressively to the creature by the Holy Spirit, or the promised Paraclete. This is the process of an *Incarnatio continuata* coming into being, not socially, but through the flowering of spiritual individuality in man. The reign of the Holy Spirit as feminine hypostasis (in Semitic tradition), and identifying itself with Sophia, is thus the vision of "the dawning of a new aeon." And that is the answer to Job.

I can remind us here only with broad strokes of the general design of an interpretation that tends to indicate beforehand the key points of a future study in which Jung's Sophiology would take its place in an overall phenomenology of Sophianic consciousness. I insisted on the connections and the differences between Jungian Sophiology and the figure of Sophia in the Spiritual figures of Protestanism (Jakob Böhme and those of his lineage—somewhat forgotten by Jung in the final pages of his book). And I continued this comparison by looking into the Sophianic school of Russian orthodoxy (Sergei Bulgakov, Berdyaev, and so on), as well as finally looking into the spiritual universe of ancient Iran. In the latter, it is important to distinguish clearly the Mazdean tradition, the Zurvanite tradition, and the Manichean tradition. These are traditions in which Evil, in any case, made its appearance before the existence of man on Earth and where Evil is never a simple *privatio boni.* The plan of this study remains, of course, on my list of things to do, but up until now it has not been possible for me to carry it out except insofar as it involves the Iranian world. This has been done in a study where the reader can henceforth become familiar with the idea of Sophia as she presents herself to the vision of ancient Zoroastrian Iran as well as to that of Islamic Persia—that is, to the gnosis of Islam in its specifically Shi'ite form.*

These precisions are recalled here only to explain the sentiments expressed by Jung with so much warmheartedness at the beginning of the letter that the reader will find further on. I have endeavored to give a maximum of resonance to the research conducted through his biblical contemplations. On the other hand, he refers to the void, the vacuum, which surrounds him, aggravated even more by this *Answer to Job*. He even goes so far as to speak of an "avalanche of atrocious stupidities."

But immediately he produces a reference that delights him. It appears right from the first pages of my article, and it leads him to the attestation of a spiritual ascendency the interest of which cannot be exaggerated.

I emphasized that Jung's book was the work of an authentic solitary individual, a man alone, and that it could only be understood by solitary individuals, those authentically alone, liberated from collective norms, social obsessions, and ready-made opinions. The whole of it has its birth, precisely, in their solitudes. Such a theology, which is not learned in manuals, seems to me to correspond perfectly to the case of this individual religion that was described with such fervor by the great theologian of German romanticism, Schleiermacher (1768–1834). It is not impossible that one day he will become once again very contemporary. Schleiermacher was the Protestant theologian who foresaw the demand for a general theology of religions and a history of religions—that is to say, a Christian theology capable of recognizing and valorizing the spiritual reality of the fact that the history of religion continues *after* and *since* Christianity and

---

*See Henry Corbin, *Spiritual Body and Celestial Earth,* trans. Nancy Pearson (Princeton, N.J.: Princeton University Press, 1977).

is not concerned only with what took place *before* Christianity.

In a spirit inspired by the *Monadologie* of Leibniz, Schleiermacher professed, in his *Discourse on Religion,* the only one to really have the "keys to the city" in a religious universe is the man for whom a central personal intuition allows the whole religious edifice to be connected to this central intuition. In contrast, "He who would not be able to construct it himself, if it had not already existed, such a person will not connect himself either to one of the existing religions, but will be constrained to produce a new one in himself." Even if he remains alone and is without disciples, his religion "has just as well a face and a given organization. It is just as much a positive religion as if he had founded a great school."

This is the quotation Jung reacted to so favorably in the course of his letter reproduced further on. He claims that Schleiermacher was, unconsciously at least, in the course of Jung's life, his *spiritus rector*—that is, his tutelary genius, his spirit guide, in short his "spiritual ancestor." This claim is also based on the fact of a very distant family connection with the great theologian. Certain pages of the autobiography allow us to appreciate the declaration made here that "the vast, esoteric, and individual mind of Schleiermacher" impregnated the atmosphere of the paternal family. In a later conversation, at Bollingen, Jung returned again to the circumstances in which Schleiermacher had conferred Protestant baptism on his grandfather, who was already a doctor.* He further he spoke of how this grandfather had been the friend of the theologian Wilhelm Martin de Wette (1780–1849), another great name in the Protestant the-

---

*See the information available now concerning Jung's genealogy, assembled by Aniela Jaffé as an appendix to her edition of C. G. Jung's *Ma vie: Souvenirs, rêves, pensées* (Paris: Gallimard, 1966), 399–400. We find in that book, in plate 22, the reproduction of a beautiful portrait of this ancestor who was already a doctor and who bore the same given names, Carl Gustav Jung (1794–1864).

ology of the time, a theology in which also the mind of Schelling
was not absent. De Wette was himself a friend and admirer of
Schleiermacher, both equally giving total superiority to the cogni-
tive scope of feeling that is presentiment, or "divination," above any
dialectical or scholastic rationalism.

And then, as Jung recalls with good reason and happily, de Wette
was one of those theologians with a sense of symbols. He willingly
"mythologized" Bible stories, using his own words. This is in striking
contrast to the tendency of certain theologians of our times who speak
of the necessity of "demythologizing" the Bible and Christianity, perhaps because they have never really understood what a myth is, or
what a symbol is, or what a living and experienced religion is, or else
it is out of a furor of infatuation for historical realism, near relative
of historical materialism plain and simple. It is not by chance that
Jung's present book opens with the affirmation of the full reality of
the Event, even and above all in the case where the event is not a physical manifestation, because it cannot belong to the empirical reality of
what we call History. Truly, *Answer to Job* can be understood only on
condition that we do not isolate it from the context of this Protestant
theology, the dramatic grandeur of which was to be able to renew
itself unceasingly, tearing itself away from the stagnation of a definitive dogmatism.

There is another point that needs to be raised. Jung's German
text presents, at moments, the affective tonality of a contained passion that is difficult to move into French. I had mentioned on certain pages the innermost vibration of a Sophianic hymn, hailing the
approach of the eternal Virgin that means a new Creation. And I
finally confessed to having reread the whole book as if it were an
oratorio. One day, its score could imprint itself on a Handel of the
future and it would end with a choir of soothing alto voices singing:
Ave praeclara maris stella. These lines motivated Jung's reference to

the genesis of the book in "illness, in fever." The terms with which he describes the musical "accompaniment" remind me of what was—alas!—our final conversation. I had asked him about the way in which he understood musical experience: its virtues as spiritual therapy, or on the contrary, threats and symptoms of disintegration when it explodes and degenerates, as sometimes it does in our times. And I had been struck by the consideration, received in response, that music has a virtue of *katharsis* (purification) only if it leads us to a *visionary* inner experience, in the strong and prophetic sense of that word.

With a touching intention, Jung wanted to write his letter in French. When, with excessive modesty, he excuses himself for the difficulties he experienced, we cannot entirely believe him since conversing with Jung in French was very easy. Perhaps, however, he would have said more if he had written in German. In any case, documents written by Jung directly in French are not so numerous and therefore the present one is very precious. We have said above that there would need to be an urgent motive regarding publication of the French translation of *Answer to Job* for us to decide to publish it. May we kindly forget what concerns the person of the recipient of the letter and retain only what it teaches us about the person of Jung and his intimate thought.

We have reproduced here the text as is, respecting, of course, the paragraphing. Beyond that we have undertaken only four or five very slight orthographic or grammatical "retouchings."*

---

*The letter was written on both the recto and verso sides of a sheet of white paper printed with a personal header and measuring 29 x 21 cm [11⅜ × 8¼ inches —*Trans.*].

Prof. Dr. C. G. Jung, Küsnacht-Zürich

Seestrasse 228, May 4, 1953

Dear Sir!

A few days ago I received an offprint of your essay on "eternal Sophia." It is unfortunately impossible for me to express to you all the thoughts and all the feelings that I experienced in reading your admirable presentation of your subject. My French is so rusty that I can no longer use it to formulate exactly what I want to say to you. But I must tell you how delighted I am with your work. For me it was an extraordinary joy and an experience not only among the most rare but rather unique to be understood completely. I am accustomed to living in a more or less complete intellectual vacuum. And my *Answer to Job* did nothing to diminish that; on the contrary, it set loose an avalanche of prejudices, misunderstandings, and above all atrocious stupidities. I received hundreds of critiques, but there is not even one of them that approaches—even distantly—your understanding that is as lucid as it is penetrating. Your intuition is astonishing: Schleiermacher is truly one of my spiritual ancestors. He even baptized my grandfather, born a Catholic, who was then already a doctor. Later, my grandfather was the great friend of the theologian de Wette who had a friendly relationship with Schleiermacher. The vast, esoteric and individual mind of Schleiermacher was part of the intellectual atmosphere of my paternal family. I never studied him but he was unconsciously the *spiritus rector*.

You say that you read my book like an "oratorio." The book "came to me" during an illness, in a fever. It was as if accompanied by grand music of a Bach or a Handel. I am not an auditory type. Because of that I understood nothing. It was only the feeling of a grand composition or rather a concert that I was attending. The whole thing was an adventure that happened to me and that I hurried to record.

I must mention that de Wette had a tendency to "mythologize" (as he said) the "marvelous" (that is, shocking) stories from the Bible. In doing so he preserved their symbolic value. This is exactly what I have endeavored to do not only with the Bible but also with the misdeeds of our dreams.

I don't know how to express my gratitude, but I must tell you again how much I appreciate your good will and your unique understanding. [. . .]*

YOURS VERY DEVOTEDLY,

C. G JUNG†

At the beginning of these pages we referred to the Eranos circle. For us, Jung's memory cannot be separated from that circle. It is remarkable that there was as well a mind similar to that of Schleiermacher, the great theologian from Marburg, Rudolph Otto, who was, originally, the *spiritus rector,* of the Eranos circle, as the organizer and animator of the circle for thirty years, Olga Fröbe-Kapteyn, used to love to tell us.

When two years ago we were called upon to say a few words *in memoriam,*‡ it was a text of Jung's that came to us for the evocation of what remains forever preserved in the invisible. A text that has for a long time remained confidential, printed in only a few copies (in the style of a liturgical text, in black gothic characters, framed with a red border), before being published recently as an appendix to the German edition of the autobiographical *Memories, Dreams, Reflections,* "Septem Sermones

---

*There is omitted here one line relating to a personal detail.
†This letter was included in C. G. Jung, *Correspondance,* vol. 4, 1951–1958 (Paris: Albin Michel, 1995).
‡See Henry Corbin, "Eranos: In memoriam Olga Fröbe-Kapteyn," in *Eranos Jahrbuch* 31 (Zürich: Rascher Verlag, 1962), 9–12. [See this same text reproduced in the appendix. —*Ed.*]

ad Mortuos" (Seven sermons to the dead) delivered under the name of the gnostic Basilides, in an Alexandria where, certainly, East meets West, but that we must look for elsewhere than on our geographic maps.

The dead came back from Jerusalem where they had not found what they sought—no doubt because they were not yet aware that they were dead. The message that reawakens among the dead is the message that awakens in the consciousness to the effect that the creature dies to the extent that it does not manage to conquer its differentiation—because the principle of individuation is the very secret of Creation. A collectivized world that rejects this principle, a world in which the individual trembles to differentiate himself, is a world that is cursed, because it condemns the creature to fall back below himself into the undifferentiated depths. That is the death of creatures and it buries them forever in this world. Here are the final lines of the message:

> Man is the great doorway through which, coming from the exter-
> nal world of the Gods, of demons and of souls, you penetrate into
> the inner world [. . .]. At an immeasurable distance there shines
> a single Star at the zenith. The Star is the single God of this
> Singularity. The Star is his world, his pleroma, his divinity. In this
> present world man is Abraxas who gives birth to and who devours
> his world. This Star is the God and the aim of man. It is his single
> God who guides him, the Singularity in which he finds repose, the
> Singularity to which tends the long voyage of the soul toward the
> meeting with death [. . .]. It is this Singularity to which man prays.
> And the prayer increases the light of the Star; it throws a bridge
> above death. . . .*

---

*This is a direct translation from the French, which is presumably Corbin's own trans-
lation from the original German. —*Trans.*

Close to forty years separate the moment when Jung wrote these lines and the moment when he published *Answer to Job*. We believe we can discern a straight path that leads from the one to the other.

PARIS, APRIL 1964

APPENDICES

1

LETTERS TO
MRS. OLGA FRÖBE-KAPTEYN

September 6, 1949

Dear Madame [Fröbe-Kapteyn —*Trans.*],

It is already a week ago today that we left Ascona with a great deal of nostalgia in our hearts. Also, it has been a week since the memorable visit with Professor Jung. We chatted together surrounded by his books and manuscripts for close to three hours. Listening to the man himself commenting on certain alchemical images and on certain texts of Pico della Mirandola was certainly the most beautiful gift he could have offered me on this first meeting. It was so cordial, so communicative and full of promise that those few hours managed to extend their full sense to the marvelous Eranos days. Thank you then from the bottom of my heart for having so happily arranged this interview. Mr. and Mrs. C. A. Meier have also been exquisite friends. We share the same hopes.

Now, we are enjoying going over in mental review moments from our Tagung. It is with very full hearts that your two "Orientals" took their leave. Be assured that the "Roundtable" is henceforth for us the center of this vast mandala in which our Iranian peregrinations have us traveling through distant outposts! And for that, thank you again. I am already contemplating in advance my "Rituals" for next summer.

In the course of this month I will send you the manuscript. And I am thinking about the end of December to send you the one for the Festschrift.

It is still agreed that next Saturday we will gather here with J. Barrett and Van Gillmor, Massignon and Father Beirnaert. We will speak of many things.

Accompanied by very affectionate messages from Stella, I send you, *chère Madame,* my heartfelt greetings.

Paris, October 10, 1949

Dear Madame,

Finally now ready for printing I am sending you the text of my two talks. I have kept them absolutely the same as they were delivered, and in harmony with the "gong" that graced me with its resonance. In conformity with your advice I have maintained the strict shortening of § 3 of the second talk. Doing so has allowed me to save nearly five leaves, but it is impossible however to condense it further since each line is already weighing very heavily. The notes required quite a lot of work— but they are all there and carry what is indispensable. There is missing only here and there the exact pagination numbers; I will add them on the proofs in Tehran where I have left my "material."

I have indicated on the small leaf that precedes everything else a few indications for the printer. Among other such indications, the idea came to me that the quotations translated literally from Arabic in the folios numbered 28, 29, 30, 31, 32/33 (in blue pencil) could be printed in small letters in order to gain more space. I have indicated that in the margin of those pages. But of course the decision rests with you if you prefer to have everything in the same font size.

We had a lively and very agreeable evening with Miss Gillmor, Mr. Barrett, Father Beirnaert, and Massignon, who outdid himself in the evocation of his memories of the Orient. We spoke of Eranos and we were all very happy.

I still think I will be able to send you at the end of December my contribution to the C. G. Jung Festschrift (the little piece from Jābir). I am waiting for the arrival of a text from Cairo, which will help me a lot.

Allow me to point out a very interesting book (about *Mensch und Ritus*) although you perhaps already know about it. It is volume VIII of the *Annales du musée Guimet* (1899) that I have just been leafing through at the Bibliothèque nationale and which is devoted to "Ritual gestures of the officiating priest in Tendai and Shingon ceremonies" from Japanese Buddhism. Striking illustration of the omnipresence of the *Imaginatio vera*!

We are taking a plane to Tehran October 30th. For a time we will be a little far from Ascona, but in spirit and in our hearts we will always be very close as you know.

Accompanied by very friendly messages from Stella, I send you, *chère Madame,* my warmest greetings.

January 4, 1950

Dear Madame,

A few lines first of all to send you our good wishes, and then to announce that the *Livre du Glorieux* (The book of glory) is finished. However, as I feel that I am already late, this short note will serve as a forerunner while the typing moves to completion. It will be on the next plane, at the latest a week from now. So don't be worried and don't lose patience. I have kept my promise.

I must confess that this little work on Jābir is one of the most abstruse things I've had to deal with. The text in Arabic is only a few pages long; I have provided a translation. However, rendering it intelligible required a serious study of the topics that it raises, for example: alchemy and Ismaeli gnosis; the three hypostases in Shi'ite gnosis; the three hypostases in the "Livre des Glorieux;" the "Balance of the letters" (a principle of Jābirian alchemy); and finally the Glorieux as an archetype. All of that fits very well with the program of the Festschrift. But it was so hopelessly complex that if I were able to finally get to the end of it, it was from the love of Eranos and C. G. Jung! And then, as you will see, where would I have been able to say all that if it weren't at Eranos? I am delighted to have had the chance to formulate these things, and to be something of an agent of connection to Arabic alchemy.

I received a microfilm from Jildakī in London that will be invaluable I think for the talks this summer. Finally, I have the impression that I will be able to condense them into two unpublished manuscripts, titling them simply "Rituel sabéen et bréviaire d'extase" (Sabian Ritual and Breviary of Ecstasy).

Here we are now entering the New Year, which allows us now to speak of the Eranos meeting in the future and not in the past. Already we are joyful about that but there is work in abundance between now and then.

With the great hope that all is well in Ascona and that all our friends are well, I repeat once again, *chère Madame,* along with friendly thoughts from Stella, my most sincere good wishes.

Henry Corbin

2

Sophia Æterna[*]

Preliminary Note: The few lines that follow here were supposed to have appeared in a book coauthored by Henry Corbin and Mircea Eliade, composed on the occasion of Jung's eightieth birthday in 1955. Three different, already published, texts were to have been included.

Alas! The proposed book was never published—as a result of circumstances unknown to us. And we owe then a big thank-you to Stella Corbin for having thus given us access to the "idea" that has prevailed— and which can be summed up obviously in the word meetings, to which Corbin was so attached. —Ed.

The title of this little book measures precisely its intention. There is no attempt to systematically outline C. G. Jung's thought in its entirety. These are "meetings" with his thought, before all else— presences of soul to soul, for which the event would have taken place regardless of the separating geographical distances but which came, repeatedly, to crown the faithful dialogues of real presence.

Two orientalists, who are also friends, united by many thoughts,

---

[*]Published under the title *Æterna Sophia* in the collection *Albae vigiliae* (Zürich: Rhein-Verlag). —*Ed.*

by the same manner of formulating and delivering the tasks of the science of religions, offer here their experience of these meetings. The tale is brief: barely enough to fill a little book. However, the texts that have already appeared not long ago and were not widely distributed have been reproduced here in very much the same way as they had been drafted in their initial inspiration. This has been done to preserve the tone of personal experience that was what motivated the authors and had them welcome these meetings in the first place.

And this is also the only motive that brings them together here. Last July, in Zürich, a solemn homage was paid to C. G. Jung on the occasion of his eightieth birthday. Many publications celebrated this event. May the honored birthday elder kindly accept the modest homage that these few pages in their turn propose to offer to him. May their restricted scope be compensated by the fidelity with which we have endeavored to specify our intentions and capture the reminiscence of memorable conversations.

Because the authors are not professional psychologists, their texts are able accurately to attest to what a stimulant the research and thought of C. G. Jung are more and more going to become for religious studies—let us say quite simply for "theological" studies, not in the denominational sense of the word, but in the sense that the word "theological" had originally in Greek.

Three texts are then brought together here. Their authors are quite aware that their texts ought to be expanded and deepened. However, we have just mentioned the value attached here to maintaining their initial, spontaneous form. Their connection will be apparent in itself to the reader. Essentially this connection has no other secret than that which pulls together each volume of the *Jahrbuch* of the Eranos circle, where the authors have many times participated fraternally, both of them, at Ascona; these pages will once again remind us of those occasions.

The first and third of these texts appeared under the signature of Mircea Eliade, in the October 9, 1953, issue of the magazine *Combat* and in *Le Disque vert* 1955 (in homage to C. G. Jung).

The second text appeared under Henry Corbin's signature, in issue number 5 of the *Revue de culture européenne* (year 3, 1st trimester 1953). It was titled as it is here, "La Sophia éternelle." The occasion for its publication was the extraordinary little book by C. G. Jung, *Antwort auf Hiob* (*Answer to Job*), which had just appeared. If we are presenting here this text without modification, it is not only because Jung's book has not yet been translated into French, nor is it simply because of the reception that the article in question received, nor is it because of the necessarily limited number of readers who were able to arrange for delivery of the publication in which it appeared. Instead, it is more because of the friendly approbation accorded by the honored birthday elder to the exegesis that had endeavored to interpret his intentions, while at the same time deliberately giving them a personal resonance. In this sense, the contemplation that led to the composition of the article was one of these "meetings" that the title of the present book commemorates.

Certainly, the reception that was accorded to the article reproduced here was not without resemblance to the reception of the book that it was examining and commenting on. It was designed to provoke the same astonishment, the same censure, the same scorn but also, in some readers, the same enchantment. At the summit of the long and poignant experience of a whole life, the psychologist C. G. Jung dared to deliberately venture into the theological domain. We all know that theology in our world has been for a long time an "exact science" and a reserved domain. That is why charging the unexpected player with "incompetence" remains the most sensible excuse for considering him vacuous.

If we are to have innovation, that is precisely what we have here. Theology must become, or become once again, a science of experience, a science whose interest concerns most directly the destiny of each individual person. Without any doubt, the research and discoveries of the psychologist C. G. Jung result in restoring to the word *theology* the taste of a science of life, and this is perhaps the result that, especially in our Latin countries, can appear to be the strangest, and seem like a veritable encroachment. But none of us lives without a theology, and most often it is unconscious. And because it is individually unconscious, theology has been set aside as being solely the business of a constituted body that pursues it according to certain standards and certain collectively fixed postulates. This is why theology can so easily undergo an integral laicization and secularization, and that in the metamorphosis we find obsessive conformism to these "philosophies of history," of which the mythology weighs still on our official problems even after their collapse.

But it is incumbent on each individual, one on one with himself, to give his own "Answer to Job." This answer will certainly be the work of his whole life, since, borrowing from the title of a recent book, it will be the message of his "first and last liberation." That the work of C. G. Jung might become for each individual a help with respect to this spiritual liberation is what we view to be its greatest worth. Its worth also authorizes us to recall the Protestant origins of his work and to do so all the more, because many Protestant readers of the book and of the article have discovered hidden in it something like a crypto-Catholicism, whereas many Catholic readers have discovered in particular a gnostic resurgence. These contradictions are inevitable; they are even welcome if they are the sign of a theological debate that interests our life passionately.

The framework within which the analysis of Jung's book was recorded here requires a minimum of amplification. *Answer to Job* has been analyzed as a phenomenology of the "Sophianic religion." We had to be satisfied with a simple reference to this religion of Sophia, such as it was experienced within Protestantism itself, with Lutheran spiritual leaders in the tradition of Jakob Böhme. In ending, scarcely were we able to insist a little more at length on its resurgence at the heart of modern Russian Orthodoxy with the Sophiology of Father Sergei Bulgakov. These references are far from covering the whole extent of Sophiology, the concept of which manifests within Christianity as well as outside of Christianity.

However, the birthday homage that we are called to participate in here leads us to overcome our regret at having to reproduce our text without the desired amplification. This will be remedied in the next German edition of this same text, which will be preceded by a sketch in which we endeavor to bring together the voices of Sophiology across the ages. Under the same title of *Sophia Æterna,* we will give the equivalent of this little book to the French-speaking reader, while making available to him texts that are not easy to access. Then, in the context of an eternal Sophiology, it will be possible to discern more clearly the resonances of the phenomenology of the Sophianic consciousness established by C. G. Jung.

PARIS,
SEPTEMBER 1955

Planned Outline for Sophia Æterna

I—Answer to Job

I. The Self of One's Self

II. *Answer to Job*

    1. The Absence of Sophia

    2. The Anamnesis of Sophia

    3. The Exaltation of Sophia

III.

    1. Kierkegaard, the Christian Job

    2. The Sophiology of S. Bulgakov

    3. The Rock of Rhages

II—Sophia Æterna

1. (Quid: Zacharias and Buisset—Bechofen and his struggle—his failure—the question of Job: Where is Sophia?)

2. The angel Daena-Fravarti (Mazdeism) (The archetype—R. Otto)

3. Sophia and Shekhina (A.T.—Kabbalah)

4. Kore Kosmou (Hermeticism—Isis—Sophia as initiator)

5. Sophia in exile (or fallen—Gnosis—Valentinians)

6. The Virgin of Light (Manichaeism)—Cathars—Acts of Thomas

7. The Shepherd of Hermas

8. Fatimah, the Radiant (Shi'ite Islam)

9. Seraphic Anthropology (The School of Jakob Böhme—Berdyaev—Novalis—Goethe—Balzac—Solovyov).

3

"Eranos"
In memoriam Olga Fröbe*

Two eminent places are now empty among us here at Eranos.

There is the place of she whom we have always been in the habit seeing here since the beginning, because it was she who addressed to each one of us, year after year, the call, the invitation to the unforeseeable coming together that constituted each one of our sessions. This place was Eranos itself in the person of Olga Fröbe.

And there is also that other place from which, for so many years, there radiated a stimulating, attentive presence: that of C. G. Jung.

Attendees and speakers of Eranos, how could we not bring together their two names, when today those who bore those names are to be found in the peace that is not of this world?

Certainly, I am not, for the moment, contemplating any scholarly comparison between the work of Eranos and the work of C. G. Jung. The work of detecting the traces in each one of us of what we have

---

*The poem "À Olga Fröbe-Kapteyn," which appeared in the *Cahier de L'Herne* devoted to Henry Corbin, issued in 1981, can be read in conjunction with this address. —*Ed.*

been able to receive from Jung's thought is something that belongs to the future.

But in that regard there is something more—something that affects our perception of the world and, along with that, the innermost part of our inner life. And it is from this point of view, it seems to me, that we can, especially today, insist on the unique connection between what we could call the paradox of Eranos and the deepest part of Jung's thought.

The paradox of Eranos! Let us recall the exquisite letter addressed a few years ago by Olga Fröbe to the editorial staff of the magazine *Du,* which was proposing to celebrate with a special issue (April 1955) the anniversary of Eranos. Refusing, as always, to respond to the question, "What is Eranos?" with a rational definition—because there isn't one—she invited her virtual questioner first of all to walk through this garden that has become, through the contemplations of all those who conversed there, a garden of the Mind and Spirit.

Slowly then, he will make his way to this conference room. He will see there the podium from which so many different men coming from all corners of the Earth have spoken during the course of thirty years now. So many scholars, each one of whom through his own research had come to a personal perspective. All together they represented so many various disciplines. How is it that, of all the voices raised here at this podium, there results an immense accord, whereas we could have feared irresolvable dissonances?

The response is held in these two words: spontaneity and freedom. Because here at Eranos we have never had the concern of being in conformance with an already-given model, the concern of some orthodoxy, because our only concern has been to go right to the end of ourselves, right to the end of this truth that, as we know, is never glimpsed except in relationship to our effort, to our integrity and the capacity of our heart. Through this liberty and this spontaneity then, we are altogether not, certainly, a unison but a polyphony of individually differentiated voices. In a time of utter confusion such as ours, something like Eranos responds to the urgency. To she who set up for so many men of science a place where they were able to be fully themselves, to Olga Fröbe, we offer a recognition that will follow her beyond this world.

If someone could appreciate the admirable paradox of Eranos, in a world and a time where all authentic truth is smothered by forces of the impersonal, where the individual trembles to differentiate himself from the anonymous collectivity—because, for that collectivity, personal individuality is very close to being equivalent to having been found guilty—if anyone could have understood this paradox—shall we say even the challenge that Eranos brought to this world—it was certainly C. G. Jung. His name is there in the fifteen volumes of our *Jahrbuch* to bear witness to that.

But here too I don't want to speak only of something that leaves purely scholarly considerations in the dark. I remember that it was from right here, thirteen years ago, that Olga Fröbe arranged for me my first interview with Jung. I remember also another interview with him following the publication of my long article on the magnificently scandalous book titled *Answer to Job*. Of course, let us not take this book as a work of biblical criticism. It is not about a technical exegesis of texts but rather another kind of exegesis: the exegesis of a soul, of his most personal inner secret.

And, thinking of this text of the soul, I believe I am permitted, on a day such as this, to refer to a text that has remained confidential although it was printed. We have just mentioned a world where the personal individual trembles to differentiate himself. This fear and lack of differentiation that is imposed on the individual—it is this imposition that is precisely the death of the human creature. And it against this death that Jung puts us on our guard in his *Septem Sermones ad mortuos,* the *Seven Sermons to the Dead,* delivered under the name of the gnostic Basilides, in an Alexandria where certainly East meets West, but that we must look for elsewhere than on our geographic maps.

The dead were coming back from Jerusalem where they had not found what they were looking for—no doubt because they were not yet aware that they were dead. The message that is able to reawaken them must awaken them to the consciousness that the creature dies to the extent that it does not manage to conquer its differentiation— because the *principio individuationis* is the very secret of Creation. A collective world that rejects this principle *per se* is a world that condemns the creature to fall back below himself into the undifferentiated depths. And this is a world that is cursed because henceforth the dead will never ever leave that world.

Let us read, translated into English, a few lines of the final message of the *Septem Sermones ad Mortuos.*

Man is the great doorway through which, coming from the external world of the Gods, of demons and of souls, you penetrate into the inner world [. . .]. At an immeasurable distance there shines a single Star at the zenith. The Star is the single God of this Singularity. It is his world, his pleroma, his divinity. In this world, here, man is Abraxas who gives birth to and who devours his world. This Star is the God and the aim of man. It is his single God who guides him, the Singularity in which he finds repose, the Singularity to which tends the long voyage of the soul toward the meeting with death [. . .]. It is this Singularity to which man prays. And the prayer increases the light of the Star; it throws a bridge above death. . . .

An Image exists, which Olga Fröbe had premeditated and which she was fond of because for her it was the symbol of Eranos par excellence. The photograph represented in fact our "Roundtable." But there is no one there. The seats, all around, are empty. The solitude is illuminated by discreet rays of sunlight that filter through the branches of a great cedar, like sunlight coming through a stained-glass window. When he saw this Image, void of any visible presence, Jung had this reflection, "The Image is perfect. They are all there."

They are all there! Even those who will never again in this world sit at this table. Let us not take this sentence as a metaphor, as an edifying consolation to remember. Certainly, there is a word that we are shy about pronouncing because there are the "taboos" of agnosticism, so readily accepted today in all its forms, and also because there are pious dogmatisms that are no less facile. However, let us speak this word: *immortality.* For if this word is a challenge, it is because it is addressed to the living, not to those who have not yet realized that they are dead.

The work of Olga Fröbe and the work of C. G. Jung are among those works that make living people. To each one of them who have preceded us on the path of light is sent the recognition and gratitude of all those who, one day or another, have been able or will be able to say, along with our poet Rimbaud:

"And at times I have seen what the man thought he saw."

Angel Logic

Michel Cazenave

We know that Henry Corbin devoted his whole life to the study of Muslim mysticism or, more precisely, esoteric mysticism from Ibn 'Arabi to Jami and from Suhrawardi to Mulla Sadra in its various currents—Shi'ite, Ismaeli, or Sufi. Now we need to agree on this word *esotericism*. Contrary to the received opinion that makes it a synonym of occultism or a doctrine of separation between the ignorant masses that remain in the grip of religious institutions and the elite of "those who know" who would like to be protected from uncouth oddities, Henry Corbin always presented very precisely the workings of esotericism for what it really was: that is, the constant effort of unveiling carried out by the mystic and the philosopher—the exploration of hidden meaning in beings and in texts, and the rigorous lifting of the prohibition of seeing, which the Fall seems to have imposed on us. In this search for the light, it is a question of upgrading the structure of any existence whatever that has its origin in the mystery of the light behind the Light. After all, the uniqueness of the Divine thus guarantees and legitimizes the multiplicity of souls in their spiritual authenticity.

We know less, however, about how "oriental philosophy" wouldn't refer so much to a concrete geography as it would to a symbolic topography in which each cardinal point represents a "climate," an essential attitude specific to the various stages of the metaphysical quest. It is in this way that, following a vocabulary constructed in metaphor and very well set forth in the very beautiful book by Christian Jambet,* a given oriental philosopher (Indian, Chinese, or Japanese) might refer to a Western construction, whereas a given Western searcher (Scotus Erigena, Eckhart, Böhme, Leibniz or a certain Goethe) might immediately appear on the contrary in an oriental domain.

That is why, very logically, Henry Corbin has not just been this specialist in Persian Neoplatonism that we know him to be. He always sought to construct elements of a general science of forms that would allow him to uncover deep points of unity among the three Religions of the Book (Judaism, Christianity, and Islam) and to strive for deep homological comparisons among philosophies, for example those of Leibniz, Swedenborg, or Novalis, and one or another thinker from the Muslim tradition.

Within this unprecedented body of work—which no philosophical initiative, it seems to us, will henceforth be able to do without—two other books bring us stunning accounts.† We see in his work in effect this metaphysical approach that looks for homologous structures in one and another system of thought without ever confusing them.

It is here once again that Corbin revolutionizes our philosophy by reintroducing in their proper places the metaphysical categories and figures that we no longer have the courage or strength to think about—categories that the evolution of European thought had oblit-

---

La Logique des Orientaux: Henry Corbin et la science des formes [Oriental logic: Henry Corbin and the science of forms] (Paris: Editions du Seuil, 1983).
†Henry Corbin, *Face de Dieu: Herméneutique et soufisme* [Face of God: hermeneutics and Sufism] (Paris: Flammarion, 1983); *L'Homme et son ange: Initiation et chevalerie spirituelle* [Man and his angel: initiation and spiritual chivalry] (Paris: Fayard, 1983).

erated in its movement of laicization. Corbin tells us that there is no space for the soul, there is no vision and participation in the one, there is no ascension through the various degrees of being except under the direction of the angel. Or should we say angels, each one of whom is specific to each one of us? It is because a "subtle" space for the angel exists that the soul, in effect, is able to develop and be led once again to its true place of existence, which is that of a placeless place, that of the imaginal world dear to Corbin and which, in the first place, gave birth to the soul that animates us.

The figure of the angel, from then on, becomes the central figure, and, borrowing from the title of another of Corbin's books, there is a profound and urgent "necessity for angelology" for anyone trying to understand our connections with the Divine—the angel being the relationship that unites us to God and allows us to pass from the stage of individual to the status of a person.

Of course, in these last two books, Henry Corbin is a hundred times richer than what we are able to suggest here. What I have tried to bring out here is the originality of a study that is at the same time a quest. It is the updating of a certain number of structures of being that will allow us tomorrow to think beyond the breach that today affects "Western" thinking. It is the opening of life to the being beyond being that will allow us to go beyond the ambient nihilism of an impoverished culture. This vision of the angel upon whom we have closed our metaphysical eyes, bringing instead a purely terrestrial look, will allow us to rethink the Divine when it rises up in our soul where it assumes a form and a face.

LA CROIX, FRANCE,
JANUARY 1984

Bibliography

Works Cited by Henry Corbin

Bouyer, Louis. *Mensch und Ritus*. Mainz, Germany: Matthias-Grunewald Verlag, 1964.

Bulgakov, Sergei [a.k.a Sergius Bulgakov]. *Sophia: The Wisdom of God: An Outline of Sophiology*. Translated by Patrick Thompson. Library of Russian Philosophy. Hudson, N.Y.: Lindisfarne Press, 1993. Originally published as *The Wisdom of God: A Brief Summary of Sophiology*. London: Paisley Press, 1937.

Bulgakov, Sergius. *The Comforter*. Translated by Boris Jakim. Grand Rapids, Mich.: Wm. B. Eerdmans Publishing Co., 2004.

Corbin, Henry. "Eranos: In memoriam Olga Fröbe-Kapteyn." In *Eranos Jahrbuch* 31 (Zürich: Rascher Verlag, 1962), 9–12.

———. "Rituel sabéen et bréviaire d'extase" [Sabian ritual and breviary of ecstasy]. Unpublished manuscript. Date unknown.

———. *Spiritual Body and Celestial Earth: From Mazdean Iran to Shi'ite Iran*. Translated by Nancy Pearson. Princeton, N.J.: Princeton University Press, 1977.

———. "Le temps cyclique dans le Mazdéisme et dans l'Ismaélisme" [Cyclic time in Mazdeism and Ismaelism]. In *Eranos-Jahrbuch* 20 (1951). Zürich: Rhein-Verlag, 1952.

Evans-Wentz, W. Y., ed. *Das Tibetanisch Totenbuch aus der Englischen Fassung des Lama Kazi Dawa Samdup Herausgegeben von W. Y. Evans-Wentz, mit einem Psychologischen Kommentar von C. G. Jung.* Zürich: Rascher Verlag, 1942.

———. *The Tibetan Book of the Dead, or, The After-Death Experiences on the Bardo Plane, According to Lama Kazi Dawa-Samdup's English Rendering.* 3rd ed. Oxford/New York: Oxford University Press, 2000.

Jung, Carl Gustav. *Aion: Researches into the Phenomenology of the Self.* 2nd edition. Translated by R. F. C. Hull. Vol. 9, part 2 of the *Collected Works of C. G. Jung.* Princeton, N.J.: Princeton University Press, 1969.

———. *Aion: Untersuchungen zur Symbolgeschichte.* Zürich: Rascher Verlag, 1951.

———. *Answer to Job.* In *Psychology and Religion: West and East.* Revised edition. Translated by R. F. C. Hull. Vol. 11 of the *Collected Works of C. G. Jung.* Princeton, N.J.: Princeton University Press, 1970.

———. *Antwort auf Hiob* [Answer to Job]. Zürich: Rascher Verlag, 1952.

———. *The Collected Works of C. G. Jung.* 20 vols. Princeton, N.J.: Princeton University Press, 1954–1979.

———. "Commentaire psychologique du Bardo Thödol (*Das tibetanische Totenbuch*)." In *Psychologie et orientalisme.* Paris: Albin Michel, 1985.

———. *Commentary on* The Secret of the Golden Flower. Translated by R. F. C. Hull. In *Alchemical Studies.* Volume 13 of the *Collected Works of C. G. Jung.* Princeton, N.J.: Princeton University Press, 1968.

———. Foreword to *An Introduction to Zen Buddhism,* by D. T. Suzuki. New York: Grove Press, 1964.

———. *Gesammelte Werke* [Collected Works]. Zürich: Walter-Verlag, 1996.

———. *Letters.* Vol. 2, 1951–1961. Princeton, N.J.: Princeton University Press, 1976.

———. *Memories, Dreams, Reflections.* Edited by Aniela Jaffe. Translated by Richard Winston and Clara Winston. New York: Pantheon, 1963.

———. *Paracelsica*. Zürich: Rascher Verlag, 1942.

———. *Paracelsus as a Spiritual Phenomenon*. In *Alchemical Studies*. Translated by R. F. C. Hull. Vol. 13 of the *Collected Works of C. G. Jung*. Princeton, N.J.: Princeton University Press, 1968.

———. "Préface à Suzuki: 'La grande délivrance'." In *Psychologie et orientalisme*. Paris: Albin Michel, 1983.

———. "Psychological Commentary on *The Tibetan Book of the Great Liberation*." In *Psychology and Religion: West and East*. Vol. 11 of the *Collected Works of C. G. Jung*. Princeton, N.J.: Princeton University Press, 1970.

———. *Psychological Types*. Translated by H. G. Baynes. Edited by R. F. C. Hull. Vol. 6 of the *Collected Works of C. G. Jung*. Princeton, N.J.: Princeton University Press, 1976.

———. *Die Psychologie der Übertragung, Erläutert anhand einer alchemistischen Bilderserie* [The psychology of transmission, explained using an alchemical series of pictures]. Zürich: Rascher Verlag, 1946.

———. *Psychologie und Alchemie*. Zürich: Rascher Verlag, 1944.

———. *Psychology and Alchemy*. Translated by R. F. C. Hull. Vol. 12 of the *Collected Works of C. G. Jung*. Princeton, N.J.: Princeton University Press, 1980.

———. *Seven Sermons to the Dead*. In *The Gnostic Jung*. Selected and introduced by Robert A. Segal. Princeton, N.J.: Princeton University Press, 1992.

———. *Symbolik des Geistes: Studien über psychische Phänomenologie* [Symbolism of the mind: studies on psychic phenomenology]. Zürich: Rascher Verlag, 1948.

———. *Synchronicity: An Acausal Connecting Principle*. Translated by R. F. C. Hull. Vol. 8 of the *Collected Works of C. G. Jung*. Princeton, N.J: Princeton University Press, 2010.

———. *Synchronizität als ein Prinzip akausaler Zusammenhänge* [*Synchronicity: An Acausal Connecting Principle*]. Vol. 4, *Studien aus dem C. G. Jung-Institut Zürich*. Edited by C. A. Meier. Zürich: Rascher Verlag, 1952.

———. *Types psychologiques*. Préface et traduction Y. Le Lay. Geneva: Librairie de L'Université Georg et Cie, 1950.

———. "Zur Psychologie östlicher Meditation." *Mitteilungen der Schweizerischen Gesellschaft der Freunde ostasiatischer Kultur* 5 (1943). Reprinted in *Symbolik des Geistes: Studien über psychische Phänomenologie*. Edited by R. Schärf (Zürich: Rascher Verlag, 1948).

Leibniz, Gottfried Wilhelm. *Discourse on Metaphysics and the Monadology*. Translated by George Montgomery. New York: Prometheus, 1992.

van der Mensbrugghe, Alexis. *From Dyad to Triad: A Plea for Duality against Dualism and an Essay towards the Synthesis of Orthodoxy*. London: Faith Press, 1935.

Neumann, Erich. *The Origins and History of Consciousness*. Translated by R. F. C. Hull. Foreword by C. G. Jung. Reprint edition. Princeton, N.J.: Princeton University Press, 2014.

———. *Ursprungsgeschichte des Bewusstseins*. Zürich: Rascher Verlag, 1949.

Nukariya, Kaiten. *The Religion of the Samurai: A Study of Zen Philosophy and Discipline in China and Japan*. London: Luzac, 1913.

Puech, Henri-Charles, and André Vaillant. *Le Traité contre les Bogomiles de Cosmas le prêtre* [The treaty against Bogomil Cosmas the priest]. Paris: Imprimerie Nationale, 1945.

Ruyer, Raymond. "Pouvoir spirituel et matriarcat." In *Revue philosophique* (October–December 1949): 404ff.

van Ruysbroek, Jan. *Selections from Ruysbroek*. Whitefish, Mont.: Kessinger Publishing, 2005.

Schär, Hans. "C. G. Jung und die Deutung der Geschichte" [C.G. Jung and the interpretation of history]. In *Schweizerische Theologische Umschau* [Swiss theological review] (Bern), July 1952.

———. *Religion und Seele in der Psychologie C. G. Jungs*. Zürich: Rascher Verlag, 1946.

Schaer, Hans [a.k.a Hans Schär]. *Religion and the Cure of Souls in Jung's Psychology*. Translated by R. F. C. Hull. Vol. 177, International Library of Psychology. London: Routledge, 1951. Reprinted 1999.

Schleiermacher, Friedrich. *On Religion: Speeches to Its Cultured Despisers*. Translated and edited by Richard Crouter. Revised edition. Cambridge, UK: Cambridge University Press, 1996.

Suzuki, D. T. *Essays in Zen Buddhism*. Boston: Beacon Press, 1952.

Works Cited by Michel Cazenave

Casenave, Michel, ed. *Cahier de l'Herne: Carl Gustav Jung* [Herne notebooks: Carl Gustav Jung]. Paris: L'Herne, 1984.

Corbin, Henry. *Face de Dieu: Herméneutique et soufisme* [Face of God: hermeneutics and Sufism]. Paris: Flammarion, 1983.

———. *L'Homme et son ange: Initiation et chevalerie spirituelle* [Man and his angel: initiation and spiritual chivalry]. Paris: Fayard, 1983.

———. *Le Paradoxe du monothéisme* [The paradox of monotheism]. Paris: L'Herne, 2003.

———. *La Philosophie iranienne islamique: Aux xviiᵉ et xviiiᵉ siècles* [Islamic Iranian philosophy of the seventeenth and eighteenth centuries]. Paris: Buchet-Chastel, 1994.

———. "La Sophia éternelle." In *Revue de Culture européenne* 3, no. 5 (1953).

———. *Temple et contemplation* [*Temple & Contemplation*]. Paris: Flammarion, 1980.

———. *Temple & Contemplation*. Translated by Philip Sherrard and Liadain Sherrard. London: Routledge, 1986.

Jambet, Christian, ed. *Cahier de l'Herne: Henry Corbin* [Herne notebooks: Henry Corbin]. Paris: L'Herne, 1981.

———. *La Logique des Orientaux: Henry Corbin et la science des formes* [Oriental logic: Henry Corbin and the science of forms]. Paris: Éditions de Seuil, 1983.

Wilhelm, Richard, trans. *The Secret of the Golden Flower: A Chinese Book of Life*. With commentary by C. G. Jung. Revised edition. San Diego, Calif.: Harcourt Brace Jovanovich, 1962.

Index

Books of Related Interest

Instructions for Spiritual Living
by Paul Brunton

Change Your Story, Change Your Life
Using Shamanic and Jungian Tools to Achieve Personal Transformation
by Carl Greer, PhD, PsyD

Christian Mythology
Revelations of Pagan Origins
by Philippe Walter
Foreword by Claude Lecouteux

Compassion and Meditation
The Spiritual Dynamic between Buddhism and Christianity
by Jean-Yves Leloup

The Sufi Path of Annihilation
In the Tradition of Mevlana Jalaluddin Rumi and Hasan Lutfi Shushud
by Nevit O. Ergin

Journey to the Lord of Power
A Sufi Manual on Retreat
by Ibn 'Arabi
Commentaries by 'Abdul-Karim Jili
Translated by Rabia Terry Harris

Hara
The Vital Center of Man
by Karlfried Graf Dürckheim

The Path of Initiation
Spiritual Evolution and the Restoration of the Western Mystery Tradition
by J. S. Gordon

Inner Traditions • Bear & Company
P.O. Box 388
Rochester, VT 05767
1-800-246-8648
www.InnerTraditions.com

Or contact your local bookseller